Maud

Maud

The Illustrated Diary of a Victorian Woman

Adapted by Flora Fraser
Introduction by Elizabeth Longford

Chronicle Books ■ San Francisco

I am indebted first to Monica Green for typing up my notebooks. Working with Elizabeth Longford, my grandmother, was a delight and an education. Anne McDermid, my agent, gave comfort and encouragement. To my sister, Rebecca, I am grateful for a lifetime of friendship on which I have drawn in writing this book. To Mollie Berkeley, Maud's daughter-in-law, and to Lorraine Wood, Maud's great-granddaughter, I also render thanks. Alison Goldingham, Martin Marix Evans, David Playne and all at Thames Head have grappled heroically with the design and text of Maud. Lastly, Robert, my husband, has been a great support.

Flora Fraser *May 1985*

First published in the United States 1987
by Chronicle Books, San Francisco

Maud was conceived, edited and designed by Thames Head Limited,
Avening, Tetbury, Gloucestershire, Great Britain

Editorial and Marketing Director
Martin Marix Evans

Design and Production Director
David Playne

Designers
Nick Allen Tracey Arnold Heather Church Tony De Saulles Nick Hand

Editor
Alison Goldingham

Typesetting by SP Typesetting Limited, Birmingham
Reproduction by Redsend Limited, Birmingham
Printed in Great Britain by Purnell & Sons (Book Production) Limited, Bristol

10 9 8 7 6 5 4 3 2 1

Library of Congress Cataloging in Publication Data

Fraser, Flora.
Maud: the illustrated diary of a Victorian woman.

1. England–Social life and customs–19th century.
2. Berkeley, Maud, 1859-1949–Diaries.
I. Berkeley, Maud, 1859-1949. II. Title.
DA560.F74 1987 942.081 86-30988

ISBN 0-87701-429-9

Chronicle Books
One Hallidie Plaza
San Francisco, CA 94102

Contents

Introduction

Diaries are kept for many good reasons that would not occur to the non-diarist. A favourite inspiration is the writer himself, who sees the intricacies of his own character as cause enough for laying it bare, day by day, throughout his life. Another attraction may be the seemingly stirring times in which he lives. Queen Victoria kept hers because she was brought up to do so; a compelling and interesting duty. One of her ladies-in-waiting, on the contrary, kept a journal in which she felt it her duty to reveal nothing of interest.

Now at last a Victorian diary has come to light which fits into none of these categories but has the most convincing *raison d'etre* of all. Begun by a young woman at the age of twenty-nine who was neither self-absorbed nor the witness of significant events, it was simply the result of having nothing better to do. Yet in its cheerful, unassuming way it succeeds in producing an incomparable picture of English middle-class life from 1888 to 1904. It is not the diary of a nobody, but of a somebody in danger of being trapped in nothingness. Fortunately for her and for us she could triumphantly draw and paint her way out.

Miss Maud Tomlinson was born in 1859, two years before the death of Prince Albert. Her father, William Tomlinson, was already fifty at the date of her birth. In fact she was the child of elderly parents and showed it all her youth. The 'Great G', as she called her father, had been a maths master at St Peter's School, York. He retired when Maud was fourteen and went to live when she was twenty-three at Sandown, Isle of Wight.

His hobby was astronomy and he became a Fellow of the Royal Astronomical Society. At St Peter's he had been head of the Civil and Military department, and his son Herbert was to be head of the Chelsea Polytechnic and a Fellow of the Royal Society. Maud's family were of no mean professional status. Yet here she was at twenty-nine, unemployed, apparently untrained (she had her first painting lesson in order to improve the illustrations in her diary) and most negative of all, unmarried. In other words she was unimportant except as a companion to her aged parents.

They were in fact older in spirit than in years. At the last minute they countermanded Maud's plan to take a holiday in Germany, even though she had already spent three shillings on a phrase book! The 'Great G' did his best to stop her from visiting the house of shy Mr von Hacht for her painting lessons, despite the fact that his sister would be present as chaperone and Maud was by now a woman of over thirty. When Maud announced her engagement to be married he was 'very upset'. Who would read aloud to him now? There is only one moment of humour provided by the 'Great G': when he receives a present of a new skull-cap knitted in – pink wool. What with his port and gout and general discouragement he was a thoroughly tiresome parent. Nor was poor 'Nannie' (her mother) much better. Indeed she could have done with a little of the pink wool herself. On the occasion when she wanted to brighten up her brown bonnet, she sent Maud out to buy her some black ribbon.

Maud pictured between her parents 'The Great G' and 'Nannie' in September 1886

Maud was the youngest girl in a family of five boys and four girls. Except for her brother Hugh, the youngest of all, she was separated by many years from the rest of her brothers and sisters. She did not feel close to any of them, nor keep up with them when they went abroad, as most of them did. There was Ernest, a schoolmaster in New Zealand, where the eldest brother also had lived until he was killed in a gun accident. Walter and Hugh were both in Australia, the one an architect, the other an engineer. Her sister Annie knew eight languages and had run her own school in Ascot, which Maud attended during her final year of schooling. Now Annie lived in Paris and wrote for the papers. Maud's sister Emily was perforce at home, having gone blind. 'Emmie' along with the 'Great G' and 'Nannie', was a candidate for Maud's reading sessions. We hear of Maud being asked to read aloud Renan's 'modernist' *Life of Jesus* to Emmie, which she found herself gabbling at top speed. Before her misfortune Emmie had taken her degree at Girton College, Cambridge, and become a medical doctor, a rare thing for a woman in the 1880s.

One wonders why she called her father the 'Great G' and her mother 'Nannie'. The name 'Nannie' usually stands for grandmother and the 'G' sounds like grandfather. I can think of no explanation except that perhaps they had both become grandparents to her siblings' children when Maud was still only a child herself. If so, Maud was born in a sense to grandparents rather than parents. It was just another aspect of being old before her time, an old maid in her twenties.

The Crab Inn, Shanklin

A contemporary map showing the Sandown area of the Isle of Wight, where many of Maud's early escapades took place

Such were her naturally irrepressible spirits, however, that the scenes she depicted of her social life at Sandown might be concerned with young teenagers, rather than women ripe for marriage. That was often the case, one finds, with Victorian womanhood. Old before their time, they nevertheless contrived to keep more than a toe in things frankly childish.

If Maud was not close to her own older brothers and sisters, she was totally involved with her friends on the Isle of Wight. The younger members of two neighbouring families formed what she often calls 'The Firm' or the 'gang', a kind of inner magic circle within the larger social group. First the Black-Barnes family of Collingbourne: Mr and Mrs Black-Barnes; Frank Barnes; Lilian Barnes, Maud's idol, sometimes known as 'Rozzie' or 'Nanie'; Evelyn Barnes or 'Steakie'; and Ruby Barnes. Then the Boucher family: Mr and Mrs Boucher; Fred or 'Noggie' Boucher, Lilian Barnes's admirer; Mollie Boucher; Jessie Boucher; 'Hoggie' and 'Shoggie' Boucher (never say the Victorians were weak on nicknames).

During Maud's visit to Datchet on her way to York she meets among others some old schoolfriends: at Datchet, Charlie Bellairs, husband of 'Tykie' or 'Toddie' Bellairs, née 'Ba' Ritchie, Maud's schoolfriend; Ted and Beatrice, relations living close by; and Uncle Bennie. At York, another old schoolfriend Lily North; Miss Kirby, Maud's old headmistress; and her sister Miss Charlotte.

Of all Maud's friends, Lilian Barnes was probably the most important feature in her life— until she met and married her widowed Colonel. Meanwhile Lilian was Maud's 'husband'. She often called her so. They frequently had to dance together for lack of male partners, and indeed Maud much preferred waltzing with Lilian to spinning round the room with most young men. Harold Pope, of Appuldurcombe, was possibly an exception, but he vanishes without comment from the story. Of course women have danced together before and since, and if Emmie Tomlinson, Maud's clever sister, danced at all, it would certainly have been with other girls at Girton.

Maud and her old schoolfriend Lily North, taken by John Noble of York in November 1888

'The Firm' and company, posing one summer's day

/laud would wring every drop of happiness out
)f visits to old friends. There was hot punch in
he Thames Valley, a walk beside the military
band at Windsor and reunions with the girls of
ner old school in York. Prince Albert Victor of
Wales, no less, turned up in York for a civic
lance and dazzled them with his famous
collars and cuffs' — not to mention that exotic
novelty, a 'tuxedo'. Maud's preparations for the
'ork visit involved nothing short of a special
rousseau, created for her by Mrs Gibbon of
Shanklin; the usual hats and skirts bought by
ner at Redfern's sales were not nearly good
enough. Maud might have been going on her
noneymoon . . .

ll the serious factors of her life and times
eem to have been kept well below the surface.
Where was the Naughtiness of the Naughty
Vineties? Maud's sole object of high fashion,
ner feather boa, was perhaps the nearest thing.
t was always up to mischief. Feather boas, as
vell as being the last word in slinky chic, were
lso a kind of link between all members of the
'ictorian sisterhood, from the immaculate
Princess of Wales to the provocative performer
of the can-can. Evelyn Waugh's mother
Catherine wore 'a lovely feather boa' at the
ellow Book Party in Soho in 1894. Not that the
ntics of her boa had any parallels in Maud's
haracter. Indeed she expended much mental
nd moral agility in deciding what was and
vhat was not 'improper'. Was it quite proper to
ccept a cup of tea from a male acquaintance
who had directed her to the boat in Portsmouth
n her way back from York? Probably not.
Would it be 'fast' to let Mr von Hacht paint her
portrait, even if he pictured her as the perfect
ype of British spinster? Emphatically yes. It was
uite all right to walk beside the band at
Windsor, but rather risqué to dance alongside a
urdy-gurdy man at Sandown Regatta, as
Georgie Jacob did, 'her petticoats flying'.

Maud turned her attention to the 'Progress of
Women' at a lecture in York Museum; but where
lse? She seems to have been no more than
mbivalent about the two 'New Women' in her
fe; her friend 'Steakie' who was the first of The
irm to ride a bicycle in a divided skirt, and
Maud's future step-daughter who was 'defiant'
bout the possibility of wearing trousers. Maud
nerself eventually took to the bicycle, glorying
n its speed and regretting that she had not
ndulged herself twenty years earlier. But when
Steakie' was found with her feet up on the sofa,
eading some modern book called *A Woman's
lace is Not in the Home*, Maud was forced to
sk bluntly, 'Where in that case is it?' In reply
Steakie' could only look mysterious. And well
he might. In the Nineties there were few
lluring professions open to girls of 'Steakie's'
ge, though the demand for governesses was
oon to exceed the supply. Despite her own
parents' restrictiveness, Maud did not wish to

'The String Band' featuring Maud, Mollie Boucher and Lilian Barnes, photographed in April 1891

Listening to a more professional band at the top of Sandown esplanade

become a convert to 'Steakie's' new-fangled ideas. Neither she nor 'Steakie' would have gone as far as Bernard Shaw who was saying: 'Home is the girl's prison and the woman's workhouse.' In fact The Firm was virtually a matriarchy, and any glossary of their colloquialisms would have had to include: 'husband-beaters' — umbrellas.

In the alien world of foreign affairs, one reference by Maud to the Jameson Raid of 1895-6 was a sufficient nod to politics. She did not need to mention the Boer War, though her men friends were constantly being swept off into Her Majesty's service. She noted the visit of the German Emperor and the review of the Fleet, but that was because it was on her doorstep and also involved royalty. Maud made two other exceptions for royal events when she mentioned the famous Baccarat or Tranby Croft case and the Queen's Diamond Jubilee of 1897. This again was partly personal, since Maud's husband and his regiment were helping to line the streets for the procession through London.

Yet Maud was living through what is now called 'The Age of Imperialism' and the 'Scramble for Africa' was in full force. Was she indifferent? Or was it not rather that she was surrounded by people coming and going to Canada, Australia, India, so that in an international atmosphere only very domestic consequences rated coverage. After all, hers was a personal record. Social and political affairs entered her active life indirectly, when she worked at the Dispensary or Coal and Clothing Club, or attended a concert in aid of the Primrose League, founded in memory of Disraeli.

'Disaster' in Maud's personal and very human diary was not war, but the dance when her chaperone packed up early or the kettle toppled over at a picnic, so that there was no 'cup that cheers'. 'A dreadful accident' was not the death of a demonstrator in Trafalgar Square but the time when someone knocked over the lamp and billiard cues, dropped and smashed his plate in the refreshment room, lost her sash in the middle of a dance so that everyone stood and stared at her as if she had lost her dress and petticoats too. To Maud, an accident was what she could see and paint — especially her own eyebrows shooting up into her head and her mouth and eyes like three round pebbles.

Apart from the 'disasters' which in fact are the staple of every good diary, cheerfulness was Maud's beacon through life. Whatever went wrong she was always in duty bound to return to 'my cheerful self'. Later she would faithfully record it with a smile, however rueful. A 'treat' could be as trivial as a call at a shop in town for ices, and unusually high spirits were registered simply by running full pelt down a hill. Sometimes there were gay doings late at night, when Maud and Lilian danced together on the Prom. Their daring made them feel 'dizzy'; but today's secondary meaning for 'gay' was never part of that cheerful kaleidoscope, at least overtly.

Religion was church-going — twice on Sundays. Maud sometimes called it 'kirk' for reasons of verbal liveliness, not Presbyterianism. Occasionally a sermon would prove 'uplifting'. Art, however, was something that Maud longed to approach more intimately, despite the aged parents' coolness towards their daughter's dreams of redecorating Fernside. Maud's taste, aspiring though untutored, gambolled ecstatically among Japanese embroideries and trimmings for lampshades, hanging draperies for the mantel-shelf called lambrequins, Dutch marquetry, William Morris sunflowers.

Skating near Sandown Waterworks was a favourite pastime

Linden Gardens, Kensington celebrates Queen Victoria's Diamond Jubilee

Mr von Hacht's painting class helped Maud to improve her natural artistic talent, she is pictured standing third from the left

Group of the "Corps dramatique"

The "Avenue" Drawing Room Datchet

"Streakie." Sept. 1893

Group taken by Mr. F. G. Playne

The Two Elevens

Tennis Club Group

Sandown Esplanade Aug. 1894

She used Mr Marcel's curling tongs to control her unruly 'mop' and could always be relied upon to produce one or other of three songs out of her repertoire at the Christmas concert: 'I love my love', 'Tell me pretty maid' and 'Greeting'. Though Maud herself was never exactly a 'pretty maid', we must rejoice with her that 'love'—and children—at last came her way, if only in her second youth and as the second time around for her dear Colonel.

Maud first met members of the Berkeley family when Bruce Berkeley and his sister Lily, children of the Colonel, came to the Isle of Wight for a holiday. Their father came later. James Cavan Berkeley was born in 1838, the youngest in a family of sixteen with a long record of services to the Empire, particularly in the Indian Army, from which Colonel Berkeley finally emerged splendidly as Major-General, C.I.E. His great-uncle had been a genius, the famous philosopher-bishop George Berkeley of Cloyne, who held that matter did not exist except in the mind perceiving it. Several witty retorts were made to him, including the couplet:

If Berkeley says there is no matter
There is no matter what he says!

Maud also, we can be sure, would have laughed happily at the theories of great-uncle George. Jim's ancestors went back to the Berkeleys of Berkeley Castle in Gloucestershire. His ancestry is interesting for another reason, illustrating as it does the enormous time-spans created by these huge families. Jim's celebrated great-uncle was born in the seventeenth century, over 150 years before Jim himself. Jim was fifty-three at the time of his second marriage, though his hair was still red rather than grey. His first wife, Anna Sophia, whose father was in the Madras Artillery, had died in 1886, two years before Maud started her diary. She left Maud six step-children. The two step-sons were both serving in India, and of the four step-daughters, the two elder women were married to officers in the Indian Army.

Sandown pier

One of these, Ethel Lyde, often came to England with her two small children. But it was Maud's two younger step-daughters who really mattered. She must somehow make herself acceptable to them. Both born in India, Lily was nineteen and Trixie seventeen at the time of Maud's marriage to their father. The other new relatives acquired by Maud were even older than her husband, her sister-in-law Lady Peile being fifty-six and her brothers-in-law Sir George Berkeley and Commander Joshua Berkeley (Uncle Jossy) R.N.Ret., being no less than seventy-two and sixty-four respectively. It all made the thirty-three year-old Maud look quite youthful at last.

Maud's husband-hunting came to a happy end in 1892, when she and Jim got married. The best man provided the necessary 'disaster' by kicking out backwards at his own and the bridegroom's top hats as they knelt in the aisle. Husband-hunting was a pursuit that Maud and her friends revealed only covertly in their games and traditional superstitions. There was jumping over candles on New Year's Eve, breaking their twigs, throwing filbert nuts into the fire, ('Burn and die, crack and fly') and of course having one's fortune told from the cards. One day Maud wrote in her diary: 'Took a solemn constitutional along the esplanade. Wondered if we would still be doing the same, five years hence.' Maud remembered that according to the reading of her cards by mysterious Madame Erazuriz, a dark, handsome stranger would soon cross her path. But could he be merely a black cat that suddenly darted across the road in front of her?

This passage vividly suggests the state of mind in which most husband-hunters existed: hope, wistfulness, disillusion.

Milly Smith, Steakie Barnes and Maud take a rest between sets

Colonel and Mrs Berkeley taking a stroll along the Sandown esplanade in 1892

The extrovert Major Brown greeting the Berkeleys on the sea-front

Jim and Maud were married on 21 January 1892, but it was not till 1898 that their first child Dorothy was born, followed in 1899 by Maurice and in 1901 by Malcolm, when Jim's second family was complete. Meanwhile Lily and Trixie had been husband-hunting under their young step-mother's guidance—and with her keen encouragement. At length Lily left for India where she married James Longridge, a captain in the Indian Army and Trixie followed her to be her bridesmaid. I cannot help wondering whether India's absorption of the whole of General Berkeley's first family did not clear the decks, so to speak, for his second. Dorothy did not arrive till between five and six years after her parents' marriage, whereas Maurice and Malcolm came quickly on her heels.

One small question remains, which seems to have some bearing on social changes in Maud's lifetime. Why did she increasingly make use of photographs in the albums she compiled for her three children—which she dutifully did—instead of continuing with the unique water-colour sketches on which her own diaries were based? The obvious answer was that as a wife and mother she was too busy. But it was also a case of the all-conquering camera. One remembers Madame Erazuriz who bought Maud and Lilian each a photograph frame before returning to some unknown destination abroad. Everyone was giving photograph frames as presents, from Princess Alexandra and her ladies-in-waiting at the end of a royal tour, to the bald fortune-teller of Sandown.

The enthusiasm for life and happiness that Maud felt is infectious. Even her sketch books reacted, becoming steadily more exuberant as the years and her youth passed, but her skills increased. Taking a page out of her song-book, we cannot fail to respond with an enthusiastic 'Greeting' to Maud's newly found diary. It has been in her family's possession all these years and deserves the kind of welcome from the world of her descendants that would have made her 'dizzy'. The problems of our world are of course very different from hers. Many of her gifts were none the less timeless: in particular her zest for life and her gift for making much out of little.

Flora Fraser, who has adapted this enchanting diary with such empathy and perception, is three years younger than Maud was when she began her writing and sketches. Yet Flora was already the author of *Double Portrait* and had begun research for a biography of Emma Hamilton when she and Maud 'met'. Not only does this illustrate the vastly changed pace in women's achievements then and now, but it also exemplifies the good fortune that always attended Maud in the end.

A baker making deliveries to the Bull Ring at Brading in 1890

Maud's new family, from left to right, Ethel, Maud, Jim (JCB), Trixie and Lily, taken at Ardath, Sandown in 1892

'Great G'

'Nannie'

Maud

Harold Pope

Cast List

London

Colonel, later Major-General,
'Jim' James Cavan Berkeley
retired soldier and Maud's husband

Ethel, Lily and Trixie
Jim's daughters

Sir George Berkeley
Jim's brother

Sir James Peile
Jim's brother-in-law

Lady Peile
Jim's sister

Uncle Jossy
Jim's naval brother

Conrad Phipps
an admirer for Trixie

Jim Longridge
Lily's fiancé

Datchet

Charlie Bellairs
husband of Maud's old schoolfriend

'Tykie' or 'Toddie' Bellairs
née 'Ba' Ritchie, Maud's old schoolfriend

Ted and Beatrice
relations living close by at Thorpe

Uncle Bennie
popular gigantic guest

Shrewsbury

General and Mrs Jackson
old friends from India

York

Lily North
Maud's old schoolfriend

Charlie Cooper
dancing partner

Miss Kirby
Maud's old headmistress

Miss Charlotte
Miss Kirby's sister

Mrs Sydenham Walker
fashionable matron

Dr Baker
Principal of The Retreat, an asylum

"Tykie" Bellairs

Charlie Bellairs

Frank Barnes

'Dovonie'

Lilian Barnes

'Noggie' Boucher

'Steakie' Barnes

'Shoggie' Boucher

Isle of Wight

Madame Errazuriz
mysterious foreigner

Colonel Jacob
affable friend

Georgie Jacob
madcap romantic

Uncle Ward
naval chum

Major Brown
keen on amateur theatricals

Mrs Hatchet
interfering matron, 'the Enemy'

Wilfrid Parker
amiable chump

Harry Maund
keen yachtsman

Fernside, Sandown, Isle of Wight

The 'Great G'
Maud's father, retired schoolmaster

'Nannie'
Maud's mother

Maud
born 1859

Annie
cook-general

Emmie
blind sister of Maud

Collingbourne Lodge, Isle of Wight

Frank Barnes
soldier, marries in New Brunswick

Lilian 'Rozzie' or 'Nanie' Barnes
Maud's idol

Evelyn 'Steakie' Barnes
bicycle pioneer

Ruby Barnes

Appuldurcombe House, Isle of Wight

Mrs Pope
haughty lady of the manor

Harold Pope
admired by Maud

Spring Villa, Isle of Wight

Fred 'Noggie' Boucher
Lilian's admirer

Mollie Boucher
spinster by choice

'Hoggie' Boucher

'Shoggie' Boucher

Luccombe, Isle of Wight

Mr and Mrs Frere
owners of a fine tennis court

Ernest Frere

Bea Frere

Lily Berkeley

General Berkeley

Ethel Lyde

Jim Longridge.

Frivols and Frolics

1888 to 1889

January 1888

The New Year began with a duty visit to Mrs Raglan-Barnes. Admired a new sofa cushion she had worked with a motto in gold thread on moss-green sateen: 'Lie still and slumber'. Could not but feel it was strikingly apposite to the occasion, as half the company was nearly asleep. Not the best of days on which to have an 'At Home'. Everyone very tired after the excitement of the New Year's Eve Dance at Mrs Hatchet's. What possessed that redoubtable matron to throw a dance, none of us can understand. There were rumours that a niece was expected from London, but it was only the old crew from Sandown and Shanklin who graced her conservatory. Hoggie, that graceless scamp, found some candles and invited us all to jump over them for luck. Mrs Hatchet was furious and declared all her domestic economy for the year ruined by this incursion into her stores. Hoggie was unrepentant and we all had a fine old time. Narrowly avoided burning the hems of our dresses, and, as narrowly, avoided knocking over all the candles.

Mrs Barnes had out a lovely tea-cloth for her tea-party, worked all over with cyclamens and honeysuckle. Shoggie Boucher, unused to such daintiness, contrived to slop his tea all over it. Thankful it was not I. As it was, my new feather boa, which I wore for the first time, got into my teacup, causing much alarm and merriment to all assembled. Lilian Black-Barnes was, as ever,

Jan. 1st New Year's Day. Sunday. Mrs. Raglan-Barnes at home. Multum in Parvo

Jan. 5th Thursday morning. Writing from dictation

Jan. 6th Friday. Shanklin Bachelors' Dance.
We are informed that our chaperone has gone off

Jan. 8th Sunday Morning
Late as usual

Sunday Evening. We went to Shanklin Ch
in a lovely Scotch mist

strong in adversity and wrung out the offending object in the kitchen sink. Fear it may never be the same again, none the less.

This winter much enlivened by the diary I have begun. The dull hours closeted with the Great G and Nannie now pass in a dreamy haze as I wait till they go to bed, and then fill my notebook. Very pleased with my purchase. Black leather with cream pages. I keep it cunningly hidden under three layers of coloured zephyr night-gowns, just in case Nannie feels tempted to pry in my drawers.

Very disturbed by Nannie's refusal to allow me to make the arrangement of Japanese fans I wanted on the overmantel in the library. She insisted the Great G would not be amused so I gave up the idea. Those piles of scrappy papers all jumbled up anyhow above the mantel lambrequin do sadden a girl's heart. Nannie told me to confine my efforts at decoration to my own room, and had some hard things to say about the state of it. She objects to the lively band of cretonne, with sunflowers worked on it, and brown velvet discs for the centres, with which I have decorated the mantelpiece. It took Lilian and me two whole afternoons to fix the sunflowers in place, so I was quite hurt by her remarks.

Small disaster when we went to the Shanklin Bachelors' Dance. Lilian and Steakie and I travelled over by train with Mrs Caldecott, a tireless chaperone who is always ready to escort us where'er we will. However, on this occasion, shortly after we arrived, we found that she had given way to a rheumatic pain and gone off home in the omnibus. Bertie Peacock broke the news to us. Lilian's presence of mind saved the day. She commanded Bertie to drive us home. A frightful kerfuffle with fans and cloaks ensued but, at 4.15 am, we thankfully reached our beds. The Great G awoke, most unfortunately, just as I was tiptoeing past his door, but I feel I smoothed things over. Escaped next day to Collingbourne, where the girls and I really let our hair down, discussing Men.

Jan. 7th Saturday.
Talking it over

Woke late on Sunday, despite stern resolutions to rise early and sew a cover for my psalter. Had to run to church, where all the congregation turned round, to my shame, on my entry. Tried to slip into a pew unnoticed, but my boa came off and festooned itself around the post of the pew. Excellent sermon, all about converting those dear little children in Africa to our Christian ways. Gave 6d, in token of my appreciation . In the evening, the girls and I went with Mr Barnes to Shanklin church through a penetrating Scotch mist. Shivered all the way home.

February 1888

Feb. 3rd
Nanie & I reflect on the grey monotony of life —

Lilian and I went for a cold, wet stamp along the esplanade. I wore my new hat with the dead bird in it. Lilian wore her jacket with the fox fur trim. Weather rather blowy. Once we reached the esplanade, it seemed a shame to turn back immediately, so we braved the discomfort of a wet bench and sat looking out to sea. None of the fishermen were out. The sea quite bare, except for a flight of gulls swooping over the rocks. Lilian and I wondered how many more times in our lives we would see this same seascape. Reflected on the grey monotony of life.

Thursday. Feb. 9th
We worked hard in the morning at getting The Odd Fellows' Hall ready for the dance in the afternoon. I enjoyed it very much but it would have been more cheerful if there had been more people.

Tiring day. Ordered eatables for the afternoon dance at the Oddfellows' Hall, and wrote half a dozen dance programmes. Played cards with the Great G and Nannie in the evening, and then went over to Lilian's to help make The Yorkshire Dish — a relic from my York schooldays which I introduced into Sandown with great success. The Barnes and the Bouchers both seize every opportunity to make it, the dish being most economical and comprising brown sugar, apple slices and a pastry case. I like to prick out a loving motto atop the whole, such as 'Enough is as good as a feast', but dear Lilian does not have the patience to deal in such finicky work.

First Wilfrid Parker came over from Shanklin to help, and then Hoggie came in, so we had a very merry time all told. As usual Lilian started absent-mindedly eating all the apples we were peeling, so we had to banish her to the drawing-room. Fortunately, Noggie called at that point, so she had plenty to do, entertaining him. Returned home tired but satisfied that the guests at the dance would enjoy their taste of Yorkshire hospitality.

Louisa came over to Sandown, and he and I walked to Yaverland and back. Looked over the Manor there, and much admired the mulberry tree growing against

one of the windows. Louisa took it into his head that here was a fine opportunity to start the first silk industry on the Island. Had to dissuade him from approaching the owner. Wandered, while we argued the point, over the lovely gardens and mossy lawns. Louisa hoisted me up on a sundial and insisted I recite 'I'm the king of the castle' before he would let me down again. Very jolly outing.

Mollie Boucher, Lilian, Steakie and I had a conference at Collingbourne and decided to improve the shining hour, which seems only faintly shining this month, with a Practising Club. Accordingly, we each repaired to our separate homes, placed a bowl of water by our respective pianos and sat down in earnest to master the instrument. I had varying reactions to my morning's grappling with the keys. Annie, cleaning the hearth, declared herself much moved by my rendition of a nocturne by Chopin. The Great G came in, while I was hard at work on my arpeggios, to say he had just started a course of reading Plato and found he was vastly distracted by my music. Very difficult, attempting to be studious when each attempt brings only reproach. Abandoned my arpeggios in favour of a lullaby by Schumann, which I hoped would soothe the Great G's mood. Heard from Lilian later that Mr Barnes made a similar protest at Collingbourne, indeed went so far as to say that the rondo she was practising in the drawing-room was no better than the caterwauling the kitchen cats made. Dear Mr Boucher, mildest of men, sat in an armchair and tapped his pipe and his foot in tune to his daughter's music all morning, Mollie reported. The Bouchers are not, of course, an intellectual family, in any sense.

Lilian and I wrapped ourselves up in rugs and shawls against the inclement weather and went for a very chilly constitutional. We were very surprised that the few friends we met did not recognize us.

Wilfrid Parker came over and took us to the Shanklin New Club, where he gave us a lesson in billiards at great risk to his life. Fear we will never master the art. Had great difficulty in remembering which ball to hit

Saturday. 18th. Enthusiasm for practising
still survives & rises superior to circumstances
— the latter consisting of a cold day & no fire,
Badminton in afternoon

next. Took tea with Wilfrid's mother afterwards. She wore a most enviable bog-oak brooch ringed about with seed pearls, but would talk of nothing but the weakness of the Earl Grey at the Club. She comes from Dorset where, it seems, they drink their tea thick and black accompanied by rock cakes. She also eyed the cucumber sandwiches with some disfavour, and persisted in interrupting our enquiries about the rules of billiards by waving her gloves in the air to swat flies she declared to be hovering over the food. Feel the Club servants were quite relieved when Wilfrid bore her away.

March 1888

Friday. March 2nd. We skated near the Waterworks in morning, but the ice was rather rotten & no one seemed anxious to be in the same neighbourhoo
as Wullie. Walked over to Luccombe in afternoon to see the Freres. Sa

We went skating near the Waterworks in the morning. I wore my jacket with the Russian froggings which I had contrived out of braid from an old frock coat of the Great G's. Rather a rumpus when he saw what I had done. Declared it was unpatriotic, as well as a shameful abuse of a much-loved coat. Mentioned, as I had been meaning to do for some time, that frock coats were now entirely *démodé* and morning coats the only possible gentleman's wear. The Great G hurrumphed and swore he would wear, at his age, what he pleased, regardless of fashion's dictates. Skating rather perilous, the ice quite rotten in places, but Alice Welsford and I managed to execute several successful glissades before we decided that widening cracks in the ice and the erratic skating of others made further ventures impracticable.

Saturday 3rd Badminton. The Neals/tea.
Sunday 4th Mrs. Willan in afternoon

& afterwards sat with Nanna, who was in bed.

Great excitement. We all went off to the Lowlands' Sale. Old Major Lowland moving off the Island, following his second wife's elopement with the under-gardener. Harold Pope led the expedition. Half Sandown and Shanklin had gathered for the occasion. Mrs Hatchet was there, commenting disagreeably on all the Lowlands' bric-a-brac and china. Major Remington tottered in and made a bid for a collection of walking sticks. Georgie Jacob appeared, looking distraught, said she simply had to have the first Mrs Lowland's collection of fans, and worried at Colonel Jacob till he agreed to bid for them. We spied, for our booty, three basket chairs from the Lowlands' conservatory. With a little cunning we cleared a space among the wardrobes and Windsor chairs and fenders and sat down firmly upon them. It seemed the best way of securing the furniture, and we were only just in time. Two burly gentlemen in bowler hats who, indisputably, came from a London furniture warehouse, advanced with heavy tread on our corner. We affected not to notice and, after some grumbled confabulation, they moved away to inspect some Chinese lampstands.

Lilian raised the point, as we lolled at our ease, that none of our respective homes stood in need of basket chairs. I countered with the motto, 'Every home needs new additions.' The Sale took so long, we eventually left Harold Pope to bid for us, and retired home. We heard next day that our bid had not been high enough, and that the burly gentlemen from London had carried off the chairs in triumph.

Poured with rain all morning. Went with Hoggie to buy two clay pipes with which, in the afternoon, we practised blowing bubbles.

Lilian and I prevailed on Hoggie and Shoggie to accompany us on a walk as far as Bembridge Fort. Saw scores of rabbits scurrying in and out of the downland and saw one cross the railway track at great risk to life and limb in the path of an oncoming train. Rain coming on, we felt duly grateful to Lilian for her forethought in bringing an umbrella. Too difficult for us all to shelter under it, so we

crept behind a 'traverse' out of reach of the cruel wind. We refreshed ourselves with enormous scones. Hoggie told us of an amusing encou
had with Major Remir
old gentleman had sh
stick at poor Hoggie a
enquired when he wa
join Her Majesty's Arm
confided he hoped rat
emulate Lord Tennyso
one of Her Majesty's p
The Major was not am
stumped off to his villa
darkly of indolent yout

Went across to the Bar
where Lilian and Steaki
feeling a trifle out of so
Barnes had been called

unexpectedly to the other s
the Island, to Cowes, where
aunt of hers had been taken
ill with pleurisy. The whole
Barnes household in a ferm
as a result. Aunt Agatha, tho
not particularly liked, has al
supported the Barnes when
were hard. Lilian owes a specially pretty garnet brooch to her and Steakie had from her, only last birthday, the entire Works of Dryden. I do not believe she has more than glanced at it yet, but the sorrow of her aunt's illness bit as deep with her as with the rest. To cheer them up, I suggested frisking round the drawing-room furniture and I fancy it had its effect. We were all so tired by the end of the fun—sadly, Mrs Barnes's curtains got rather ripped in the proceedings by one of the piano legs—that Aunt Agatha was quite forgotten.

Telegram from London to say Cousin Ethelred, a revered hermit relation, had got married to his housekeeper and was bringing her to the Island for the honeymoon. Nannie became most agitated and wondered whether we had not better invite them to stay. I reminded her that the last time Cousin Ethelred had ventured out of his world of maps and books to pay us a visit, he had upset the Great G dreadfully by borrowing a good proportion

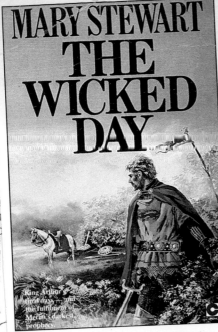

of his library to read at breakfast and marking his place with rashers of bacon.

The new Mrs Arbuthnot, however, a most dignified adjunct to the family. Gave me many tips on ways to conserve tea supplies

(mix in some sage leaves) and showed a lively interest in all the Sandown inhabitants we saw. She confessed to me she had not been out of Cousin Ethelred's house on a party of pleasure in the nine years she had looked after his house. Suggested that she come with me to Collingbourne and blow bubbles with the girls, but she preferred to return to the hotel. Went with her in the afternoon to Ryde. She had a fancy to buy some lace and Cousin Ethelred was still too unwell after the crossing from Portsmouth to accompany her. Very wet. Mrs Arbuthnot was wearing a new pair of kid boots, though I had advised her the Island weather demanded goloshes. To preserve the fine leather, we had to spend most of our time darting from one warm and dry emporium to another with the utmost celerity. Returned, piled high with parcels, to Mrs Arbuthnot's satisfaction.

Deposited her at Cousin Ethelred's sick-bed and came home with a firm resolve to sort out all the books in the Great G's library. Busy arranging them in order of subject, wondering whether the old mathematics books from St Peter's might not be profitably consigned to the attic, when the Great G came home unexpectedly from his meeting at the organist's. It seems the books were arranged in a particular sequence, in a

Evening. Sorted the books & Ended up with a row.

precise and unalterable system known only to him. My efforts had been in vain. Sat by the fire and cried.

More visitors. Dearest Toddie and Charlie have come to the Island. They are not staying with us. Relations between Charlie and the Great G have never been good since Charlie, in a fit of high spirits, pushed the Great G round the garden in a wheelbarrow, when he was courting Toddie, and inadvertently let him slip into the compost heap. Besides, both Charlie and Toddie have a liking for champagne which is not easily gratified at Fernside.

Went to Ventnor by the 12.25 pm train to have lunch with them at the Marine Hotel. Both on very jolly form. Told me they have both taken up riding at Datchet, and now roam the fields round Windsor with great abandon. Toddie confided to me that part of their object in coming to the Island was to make up the row with the Great G for my sake. At present, I am not allowed to visit

~~Monday~~. Tuesday 27th
In the morning we wandered about on the "trail" of the "new Cousin"
afternoon in Ryde: Snow & Rain. Wet through.

hem. Felt doubtful when asked o mediate, but an extra glass f champagne made me feel nore confident.

"Such is Life"

Delicate negotiations with the Great G. Nannie, naturally, eager to see Toddie. She was always a favourite among my schoolfriends. So first we talked of Toddie coming alone. I begged the Great G to remember the Christian message of goodwill to all men and reconciliation at Eastertide. He relented with an audible grunt and, the result is, Toddie and Charlie are coming to visit on Saturday. Nannie is beside herself with delight, and has instructed Annie to bake a rich variety of cakes and mixed biscuits to celebrate the occasion. Rushed over by train to Ventnor to break the glad news. Charlie less enthusiastic than might have been hoped. Though Toddie hushed him, I distinctly heard him mutter that he was doing the old goat the favour, not the other way round. Recited the motto, 'Little birds in their nest agree', to try and calm troubled waters.

Today they met, and it was as if Toddie had never been away. The Great G opened his arms wide and embraced her with great and touching affection. Tears were in all our eyes. Charlie stood back till he was summoned by the Great G to shake hands, then advanced and spoke the thrilling words, 'Sir, may I ask your forgiveness?' We waited with bated breath for the reply, but the Great G, rather disappointingly, only hurrumphed and returned no answer. Still, we all enjoyed Nannie's tea.

Wednesday. 28th Had tea with Mrs. Jones; & met Toddie, Charlie & Mrs. Barley as they passed through Sandown by the 7 train on their way to Ventnor.
Thursday. 29th. Went to Ventnor by the 12.25. Had lunch with "THEM" at the Marine Hotel. Home 5.25

a poor attempt at portraying my state of mind during the meeting

They meet. Saturday 31st March.

Good Friday. Went to Ventnor by the 3.30. Watched a coach-load of wet people disembark. Stayed dinner with "THEM"

Saturday. 31st March. Toddie & Charlie came over to Sandown in afternoon.

April 1888

Went to Ryde with Lilian and Hoggie. Did a lot of shopping. Bought, besides darning wool and slippers for Nannie, the most enchanting beaded bag, with Mrs Pope's afternoon dance in mind. Hoggie laughed at my vanity, but I feel appearances are of the greatest importance when visiting such a house as Appuldurcombe. Mrs Pope always so very well dressed. Noticed, last time we went to Appuldurcombe, she bent a beady eye on Lilian's hat. The veiling had got a trifle torn after a tangle with some brambles on the way.

A very jolly hop. Harold Pope a consummate host, though I feel he might have taken greater care when writing on our programmes. He and the Nicholson boys contrived to cause us great unpleasantness by writing their names on Lilian's and my programmes, and then handing us the wrong ones. The result was, we ended by getting engaged to several partners for each dance. Nevertheless I enjoyed myself greatly. Feel that Mrs Pope looked on with approval when I danced a third *valse* with Harold. Unfortunately, I fear events later in the afternoon served to mar the good impression I had made. I was standing by Agag on the roof-top, looking out to sea and enjoying a breath of fresh air after a polka, when he suddenly took it into his head to throw a mat playfully on to Wilfrid's head, whom he spied below. As I leant over the parapet to enjoy the joke, my eyes locked with Mrs Pope's. She was standing, stiff as a poker, and holding a cup of tea, more than half of which had slopped all over her dress. A hasty retreat seemed to be in order.

Forgot my uncertainty about the propriety of Agag's act, practising my song for the St Helen's concert with Hoggie's violin. Lilian has encouraged me lately to think I have some kind of voice, and I plan to make my debut with Gounod's 'Tell me, pretty maid'. Lilian is not herself musical, but she is always very encouraging to others. She will stand and turn the pages of the score for Noggie, when he is playing his violin, for hours. Steakie is going to perform at the concert. She is a most accomplished pianist, though sometimes the music carries her away into fabulous flights of fancy, and she ends up spread-eagled across the piano with her nose on the keyboard.

Went to Ryde with Lilian and had ices at Beti's. There were a great many customers, including a very rowdy family from Portsmouth who had come over for the day and were sitting, disconsolate, over the remains of tea with scones. The children were twisting and turning in their seats and longing to go home, as far as we could see, but the poor old father and mother looked too dispirited to make the effort to take them anywhere. One of the children came and asked us for a penny to buy an ice, and, though do not wish to encourage begging, I obliged to keep the peace. The other child then came up and kicked me, to my astonishment. Father of the party came up, cap in hand, and cuffed both offspring. In effect, a brawl was close at hand. Lilian and I made good our escape, deeply shaken by the experience.

Watched from the Barnes's drawing-room as the Hearse drew up to take the Great G and Nannie out for a morning's drive. They very sweetly offer, always, to take me with them, but the progress of the Hearse is so lamentably slow, and Mr Slingsby the driver, so dreadfully inclined to

Saturday 14th Mrs. Pope's Afternoon dance. Agag amused
himself by playfully throwing a mat onto Wilf
head, who was on a balcony below.

Wednesday night's practice

Friday 20th. Heard from Mr. Green & Rag. Barnes that the Primrose Ball the night before had been a failure. Watched from the Barnes's drawing-room the start of The Great G. & Nannie for a drive in "The Hearse"

lk, I prefer to walk. Frolicked readfully at the Barnes's, once the arents had gone.

ur concert a great success, ough Harold Pope did not ome over from Appuldurcombe, my sorrow. I was granted an ncore, which I never dreamt ould happen. Fortunately, I appened to have rehearsed with oggie an extra melody, 'Fiddle nd I', so I sang that and, remarkably, was applauded even more. Felt quite dizzy with the excitement, and bore with equanimity Lilian's cavil that my sash had drooped unbecomingly throughout the performance.

Series of peaceful days. Gathered primroses in Centurion's wood to send to Mabel's hospital. Went to hear the nightingales sing in the Lynch wood. Played tennis at the Social Club.

June and July 1888

Dr Hunt has been worriting at us for some time to come for a sail in his boat. He is boyishly proud of it, and thinks it the finest vessel on the Island. Could not disappoint him, though, personally, I think Harry Maund's Wonga the finer boat. Put on our boaters and set merrily off on the ocean wave. Only just escaped collision with another craft.
Dr Hunt was outlining to us the evidence he had given at a murder trial in Devon, and was so excited, with his talk of forceps and autopsies, he quite failed to register the other boat come sailing down on us. Only Gruffie's presence of mind saved us.
He grabbed the tiller, knocking poor Lilian's hat off in the process, and brought us about. It was quite shattering to nerves already frazzled by the sea air. What would we do without our brave boys in the Forces? Recovered our spirits, with an al fresco tea at Dr Hunt's. He lost his spectacles and could not serve the tea, but his housekeeper obliged. Dear Mrs Crowley, she can hardly see, either, and first the tea-caddy and then the tea-strainer went missing, but it was all served on pretty blue china wreathed with convolvuli and rosebuds so the effect was pretty, if there were no tea-leaves in the tea.

A most woeful experience today for Annie. She had been dusting behind the wardrobe on the upper landing, when she saw something small and black scurrying across the floorboards. It was a beetle, she swore, and the screams with which she alerted the house to the fact testified that there was indeed some insect trouble overhead. Annie covered her head in her apron and burst into tears. Nannie came out to calm her, but tripped over her knitting and the Great G emerged from his library in a towering rage and threatened to dismiss poor Annie unless she ceased her hysterics.

Desperate measures were needed to restore peace in the paternal home. I flew down the road to find help. The Lamb seemed the friend best suited to help, with his interest in lepidoptera. He is often to be seen out with a butterfly net on the sands beneath Sandown. By a miracle, he was at home, busy sticking stamps into an album. He told me he had given up lepidoptery, but would be glad to help out as it was a crisis. We steeled our nerves and carried a large bottle of poison and a guttering candle up to the upper floor. Annie emerged from her room to make more lament about a house where beetles ruled, but I banished her with a look.

The Primrose Concert at the town hall was something of a success. I am growing quite accustomed to performing in public. I gave the audience 'I love my love', and I do not think any of them guessed how near I came to abandoning the piece. Shoggie and Noggie thought up the prank of removin the sheet music from my case, a fact that I only discovered when was waiting in the wings. Lilian, like the angel she is, flew to my support and upbraided the boys in a fierce whisper till they handed back the stolen goods.

Quite hot for the first time this June. Went out in the Wonga as far as Shanklin. Then, as the win was so contrary, Harry Maund, whom we had taken up with us, got into the dinghy and rowed himself home to Luccombe. Looked on Shanklin sands from our bobbing boat and thought o Mr Dickens's book, *Our Mutual Friend*. Mused on the peculiar inspirational qualities of the Island. So many great writers hav lived and worked here, pre-eminent among them, of course, Lord Tennyson.
Sadly, though Lilian and I have made many a foray to Farringfor never yet chanced to meet the gre man. Did once see a tall, stoopir figure clad in an Inverness cape and sporting an alpenstock, striding, head down, through the village street. Thought of accosting him, speeding down the road on 'feet like jewels on a English green'. Fortunate I did not. A lady in the tea-room later informed us, in hushed tones, that my poet was really a distinguished Swedish naturalis called Dr Lindström. The Shanklin cliffs, awful in their majesty, were coming perilously near as I was musing. Persuade Hoggie to turn for home.

July

Mollie Boucher came over with some most interesting intelligence. She and Noggie and Shoggie have hatched the plan of a Sketching Party. We are all to go to Alverstone Mill, and have tea by the banks of the River Yar. I provided the kettle, Lilian and Steakie brought biscuits and scones and Alice Welsford brought that invaluable aid to every picnic—an umbrella. We met the new vicar of Yaverland on our way over. He was visiting poor Mrs Marjoribanks at her cottage in the woods. More properly, that is our vicar's province, but there has been a hue and cry.

Mrs Marjoribanks was seen boiling a fowl at dead of night, the night before the farmer's cows in the next field fell ill. Dark deeds are suspected, and our vicar has had the strongest representations from the sterner of his parishioners that investigations ought to be made.

Meanwhile, poor Mrs Marjoribanks has herself fallen ill with an inflammation of the leg, and the new vicar from Yaverland is the only mortal being who will go near her, Lilian and I consulted in whispers whether we ought not join him, but sounder counsel prevailed. We left him to his mission of mercy and proceeded on our way. In the very next field, we met a monster of a cow, which made Alice and me quail with fear and regret our decision not to go with the man of God.

The Boucher boys were too busy arguing about whether the cow was a Friesian or Guernsey to protect us. We had to sidle past its baleful glare by ourselves, muttering, 'How now, brown cow', as a charm to fend off attack from its wicked-looking hooves. Lilian and Steakie, having lived on the Island all their lives, treated Alice's and my fears with disdain. Pride comes before a fall. Lilian was so busy describing to Noggie the nightingale's song she had heard in the wood earlier in the year, she missed her footing on the stile and fell over in a heap in the mud. Luckily, she saw the funny side of it.

Lovely picnic. Made a tolerable sketch of the Mill, after watching Alice Welsford lay out her drawing. Her lessons from her father's art master colleague at Harrow lend a distinct grace to her work. Would love to have sketching lessons myself, but quite sure the Great G would consider it a waste of money. So far, thirty-two shillings in my Penny Box. Thought of secretly approaching one of the artists on the esplanade, but Lilian persuaded me that would be

Wednesday 11th This is what our sketching party degenerated into. Very cold. Snow at Portsmouth
in the morning
Thursday 12th Club day, but no tea for the simple reason (so far as we could make out) that Major Brown had gone to a pic-nic
Friday 13th. Tea with Mrs. Boucher–

'fast'. Dear Lilian has no taste for sketching herself. She inclines towards needlework as being the more ladylike accomplishment. On this outing, she did not even bring a sketch-book, in fact, but pored over my shoulder all afternoon, making helpful suggestions.

So enthused by the success of our first Sketching Party, ventured out on another expedition.
Very cold. Heard from Mrs Hatchet, whom we met on the Prom as we were setting out, that there was snow at Portsmouth. Decided in favour of nearby Culver Cliffs for a picnic spot, instead of going further afield. Would never have thought it was high summer.
Sat on the sands and shivered our way through cups of tea and toast grilled ineffectually on a pile of sticks. I wore my new hat with the veil, which rather incommoded my attempts to eat and drink, but was declared very fetching by Shoggie, to my great pleasure.

Discussed with Mollie whether we would prefer to live off the Island, the question having been brought to mind by the sight of some very raffish day-trippers. They came and paddled very close to where we had established ourselves, the men of the party exhibiting most hirsute legs. We were rather taken aback by the freedom of some of their expressions, as they tested the water, but their uninhibited pleasure in the sea and the sea-shanties they sang as they bathed warmed our hearts.
Only when they brought out black bottles which seemed likely to contain fearsome alcohol did our party deem it wise to move away.

A quiet week. Tennis party at the Fardells', tea with Mrs Boucher and a Bachelors' Dance at the Shanklin Institute. Wore my white again. A moderate success. Steakie danced a great deal and her hair came down on several occasions. Fortunately, I had my pins with me. It caused great amusement to the Boucher boys to see us mussing each other up.

Nannie, the Great G and the Lamb all went away by the 10.45 am train today. They are going to Freshwater for a summer holiday, so I am left in sole occupancy of Fernside—with Annie, of course. Celebrated my independence by rehanging the corner bracket in the library. Unfortunately it fell on my head, just as I thought I had it fixed. Still, no bones broken. Just a little bump on my crown. Went for a lovely walk with Lilian along by the cottages near Culver Cliffs. Thought of the years to come of similar walks and wondered whether we would ever have our own homes to return to.

Ought to have gone to the Shanklin Spinsters' Picnic.
Bea Frere was particularly eager we go, but rain prevented it. Rather thankful, as I have been to a number of Spinsters' Picnics this year, and they lack a certain *élan*. Noggie and Shoggie declared they would come and hang the picnic about with insects and spiders if it came off, so doubly relieved it did not.

Sauntered out in our Hats, at last. Summer, we hope, has really arrived. We wore the white washing silks and Lilian twirled a parasol along the Prom.
We judged that our hats outdid al

Sunday Evening. Nemesis, in the shape of a thunder-storm, pursued us, & we had to shelter under Skew Bridge, on our way from Shanklin Church —

he others on display. I had piled vhite linen bows atop a basket of cherries on my hat, which both gave me some extra height and was calculated to attract attention. Met Wilfrid Parker, over rom Luccombe, who invited us both out to tea — on the strength, feel, of our hats.

Saturday 21st Shoggie going round to say the "Party" is off.

Went to the Tennis Club, and Lilian and I challenged Bea Frere and Alice Welsford to a match. They beat us, as usual.
Alice swears she has never been taught to play, but we are all convinced she has secret lessons from the Harrow coach. Wilfrid Parker is a friend of the Welsford family and told me, in confidence, that the last time he went to stay at Harrow, he spied Alice on the school court grimly practising at six in the morning. She denies it entirely, but I thought a blush mantled her cheek as she spoke.

The Firm (Lilian, Steakie and I) persuaded Gruffie to come with us in the evening to Shanklin church. Noggie and Shoggie declared one service quite enough for them, and preferred to play football. Gruffie, being the son of a vicar, has more regard for things spiritual and gladly accompanied us. We wore our Hats again, determined to celebrate the summer. Saw a variety of friends in church, also old Mrs Etteridge and her grandchildren. They sat in a most unruly row in front of us. One of the small boys was sucking sweets throughout the service, and the youngest girl fiddled continually with her prayer book. But every time Mrs Etteridge glanced along the pew to see if they were behaving, all the children suddenly became as quiet as mice and produced seraphic smiles. Their true natures were revealed outside the church, when one of the boys took it into his head to start jumping over the gravestones. Poor Mrs Etteridge looked as if she would die from shame.
Her daughter, whose children they are, married an undertaker, which may explain the child's interest.

On our way back to Sandown, Nemesis overtook us in the shape of a thunderstorm and we had to shelter under Skew Bridge. I was vividly reminded of Mr Dickens's tale, *The Railwayman*, where a ghostly figure with lamp in hand haunts the railway line.
Thunder crashed and lightning streaked above our heads.
Lilian fell to wondering what would happen if the bridge fell about our ears. Steakie, practical as ever, said we should be thankful if no train came roaring through the tunnel. Gruffie and I felt so discomposed by these reflections, we voted to continue on our way, though the rain was still sheeting down. The Island habit of carrying an umbrella, come rain, come shine, proved our salvation and we reached home, tolerably dry.

August 1888

The Fardells' picnic ought to have come off today, but the weather was impossible, so we stayed in and made attempts to occupy ourselves with embroidery. I am intent on decorating a fire-screen for Nannie's room. Lilian has a bolder scheme. Trailing clouds of glory, she hopes to cover yards of some old velvet with satin stitches and drape it over the door as a *portière*. We tried it in position, but were surprised by Mr Barnes coming in unexpectedly. He got desperately entangled in the folds, and emerged red in the face and, for so saintly a man, very vexed. Said he preferred doors as God had made them, uncluttered by newfangled festoons and drapes. Lilian tried to argue the point, but Mr Barnes strode off without delay to his book-room. He reads the Psalms when life becomes too trying. Cannot doubt but that he turned to them on this occasion.

The Fardells' picnic came off today. Lovely sail round to Whitecliff Bay. Had to be carried out of the dinghy. Picnic very good fun.

At the Bazaar

Called on the Popes. Harold was out playing football, to my chagrin, but Mrs Pope gave us tea. Much admired her china, lovely blue-and-white Spode. Wafer-thin slices of buttered bread were very welcome, too, after our long walk. Mr Pope came in while we were at tea, and Lilian was daring enough to engage him in conversation. The result was, he offered to show us all over the grounds. We passed beneath every species of tree that has ever been invented, Mr Pope providing a mine of information on each sprig and branch. Only the thought of Harold's approval to come kept me from darting back to the house. Feel it would be dreadfully hard to spend much time with Mr Pope. He seems to have little in his head but the names of evergreens. Wonder if I could ever come to care for a garden quite as large as the one at Appuldurcombe. Discussed the parts we are to play at the Bazaar.

Fancy our costumes were a success at the Bazaar. Lilian went as one of the 'three little maids from school'. She rifled Mollie Boucher's collection of Japanese paraphernalia for the purpose, and sold a hotchpotch of items, Benares brass pots and all, from a tent emblazoned, 'Orient to Occident'. The best booth was 'Ye Old Flourre Shoppe'. Longed to buy a very pretty collection of ferns they were selling, but judged Nannie would consider them unhealthy in the home. Compromised and bought a charming pen-wiper in the form of a water-lily. Neither Steakie nor I had time for many purchases. We were rushed off our feet, providing tea and refreshments for the teeming hordes who attended the Bazaar. Both of us were dressed as national flags. It was a quaint thought of Mrs Pope's which had unexpected results.

·teakie was wrapped in the :gyptian colours and one more han usually cheeky boy ddressed her as 'Pharaoh'. wore the French tricolour, and vas glad to do so. I have always een a great admirer of ·onaparte. Several customers for ea mistook me for a French girl nd addressed me in that anguage. Steakie and I were mused, and with one gentleman carried on the joke. I answered, Certainement, au citron ou au ait?' when he asked for tea.

pinsters' Dance. Danced with lice Welsford several times. he is always much in demand as partner, knowing all the new ariations on the *valse* that come om London. Plodded round the oor with Bea Frere. Sometimes vonder if her mother ever ctually arranged dancing essons for her. Danced the polka, s usual, with Steakie. Both our ashes came off in the xcitement. Two *valses* with dear ilian and then, as we had much discuss, she came across to ernside to sleep with me.

She ran across the road very inadequately clad in a 'kaimono'. Mrs Hatchet was outside her front door, inspecting her tobacco plants by the light of the moon. Lilian said her bushy eyebrows shot up to her forehead.

Went to 'Los Altos' in the afternoon. Played 'Aunt Sally'. Lilian and I both failed, the whole afternoon, to knock Sally off her perch. Hoggie and Wilfrid Parker were most scathing. Fortunately, Mollie Boucher emerged from under her umbrella—where she had been mouldering most of the day—to restore honour to our ladies' side. Wilfrid seemed very distracted. I pressed him, over tea, for the cause of his distress. Seems two farmers had a dreadful dispute about a prize pig belonging to one of them.

The other swore it was his, and that it had been ripp'd untimely, as a piglet, from its mother's pen. Now that it was winning prizes all over the Island, this second farmer suddenly rediscovered an

30th Aug. - Thursday!!
Mr Heywood preparing the camera for the photo.

The Last of Frank - Friday - Aug. 16th

interest in it. Poor Wilfrid, who is landlord to both farmers, has had to adjudicate the whole and he knows next to nothing about matters agricultural. Pigs are to him what spiders are to the careful housewife—a matter for wonder and consternation. Advised Wilfrid to keep his head buried in his Latin texts.

Wilfrid seemed still very perturbed at the Sandown Tennis Dance. Not a dazzling event. I wore my white, as usual. All rather tired after watching the Regatta at Ryde yesterday.

Went to the Club, and took a photo of Lilian with Mr Heywood's camera. She took one of me.

September 1888

Rain and storms all day. Went to Christchurch in the evening. Very good sermon. Lilian and I shivered outside afterwards, waiting for Nannie to finish instructing Mrs Brighton in the art of flower-arranging. Could tell from the look on Mrs Brighton's face that she was not at all grateful for the information. She has lovingly polished and decorated Christchurch as long as I can recall.

Went for a breakfast picnic at the end of the pier. After breakfast it began to rain and we played games till it cleared up. Major Remington strolled by, taking his morning constitutional, and was very nearly inveigled by Lilian into joining us. His dog got in among our legs and caused havoc, however, after which we felt considerably less warm towards him. My new tea gown was completely wrecked by Sandy's muddy paws. Lilian told me I had been extremely unwise to wear it when it was evidently coming on to rain. Thought her most unfeeling.

Went on a Company picnic to Carisbrooke castle. Twenty-one of us went, including all the Bouchers and both Hargroves. Ethel looked very odd, in a poplin bodice which fitted very badly on her bustle. Thought of the sad death of Charles I's fifteen-year-old daughter while she was in prison here. Looked for the window from which her father tried to escape. Hoggie insisted he had found the one, but I doubted. We all crowded into the room where Princess Elizabeth died. Felt most affected

Thursday. 6th Sep.
Breakfast pic-nic at the end of the pier. After breakfast it began to rain, & we played games until it cleared up. Club Tournament in the afternoon. Nanie won. Fearfully cold again.

Saturday 15th Sept.

(E. H. & Mr. Baker playing "Jestia")
Mrs. Meek
C. Meeres
Sturgess
Alice
John } Neal
Rozzie
Evie
Harold } Barnes
Miss Baker
Mr. Baker
Ethel
Ida } Hargroves
Winnie Hopkins
Mr. Gibson
Mr. Berkeley
Fred
Jessie
Lady Betty
Charlie
Moses
Friday. 14th Sep. A "Company" Pic-nic to Carisbrooke Castle in the afternoon. 21 of us, including both Hargroves!! Lovely day & beautiful mild evening.

would have liked to muse in solitude a little, but Hoggie kept up a stream of jokes. Fear he rather shocked some Scottish pilgrims, who had come to inspect the site of their former monarch's resting-place.

Small Regatta at night. Ventured out, with Nannie's cashmere shawl warmly wrapped round me, and watched, with Lilian, as the boats bobbed on the sea and the children on the esplanade waved Chinese lanterns. Throngs of people still here. The summer holidays seem never-ending this year. Impossible to get a book one wants from the library. All out to the visitors.

Sat on the sand in the morning, and listened to the band. Wonder if it is true that they blacken their faces with burnt champagne corks—what would the esplanade be without them? Very unfair of the Great G to object to them on the grounds that they constitute a public nuisance. A pleasure to listen to their banjos and jolly tambourines. They played again in the evening, so Lilian and I had a quiet little *valse* together on the pier.

For it reminds us so
Of winter days we used to know
Only a few short months ago "
And half-forgot of late!!!

First bad day for a fortnight. The Firm (Lilian, Steakie, and I) sauntered out for a constitutional and met a bathing-machine in Fitzroy Street. Sign of winter. Resolved to swim a great deal next summer. Too busy with tennis tournaments this summer. Lots of tennis all this week, and evenings on the strand. All the old winter people come out of their lodging-houses in the afternoons, and sit, arrayed like ninepins, along the benches. Felt very sorry for their poor infirm limbs as we danced along the strand.

September drawing to a close. Put out my warm tennis dress, a bargain from Mr Redfern's in Cowes, serge and wool. Alice Welsford gone back to Harrow. Louisa and his mother back from their jaunt abroad. Brought Louisa along to the Arcade, where we all had tea while the rain and the wind roared outside. Mr Bruce Berkeley, here to recover from an Indian illness, introduced a most exasperating new game. Could not follow the rules at all. Lilian tried to explain them to me, which only added to the confusion. We ended up throwing all the cards in the sea.

Saturday. 29th Boat in morning with Steakie "Sparrow" (Louisa) & Mr. Berkeley. In the afternoon we had to postpone it till Monday on account of the rain. Mr. Berkeley my partner. When the rain ceased we went down to the Arcade & had tea.
an a "donkey" tournament
Mr. Berkeley introduced a new & particularly exasperating game.

October 1888

Louisa and I took on Noggie and Lilian at the Club. Noggie was his usual clowning self. He brought out his bandana from his pocket at one point and started chasing Lilian around the court with it. We all shrieked. Louisa takes his tennis dreadfully seriously. I had to concentrate hard to remember the score, while, all the time, I was dreadfully diverted by Noggie's antics on the other side of the court.

Walked to Yaverland with Lilian and Louisa. Tea at Collingbourne afterwards, and then Lucy Gates arrived to stay with Lilian.

She had a very fetching hat on, decorated with beads and feathers. Not sure whether she made it herself. Felt it would be tactless to enquire. As she and Lilian had much to discuss, returned to Fernside. Spent a quiet evening turning out my wardrobe, with thoughts of the visit to York to come.

To St Saviour's in the evening. A fine frosty night. Encouraged thoughts of piety. Thought ahead to my visit to York during a lengthy sermon, came to and found all the congregation on its knees and me left like a maypole.

Hurrying home, almost ran into the plane tree in front of Fernside, so busy thinking of all the resolutions I would put into practice next Sunday. Determined not to become like the old Jarrett aunt, who no sooner reaches her pew than she is asleep.

To the Bouchers for tennis. Shoggie, as ever, a most enthusiastic host. Pressed us to play far more sets than we intended. Partnered Wilfrid, who, absent-mindedly, directed a ball at Mollie Boucher's head. Ructions. Ate a lot of green apples, and felt distinctly unwell.

Saturday 13th Tennis, apples and tea with Shogg
The Ant took photos of the back & front of the house

So much to do, so many farewells to make before I leave for York to visit my old school haunts. Have had Mrs Gibbon working for me all this week. She is making me a dress with puffed sleeves and a sash for the winter dances, and some new bodices and skirts for every day. Been poring over *The Lady* for ideas all week. Saw a wonderful picture of Madame Patti in a concert dress, embroidered with forget-me-nots, and trimmed with a sash of leaf-green velvet. Dreamt I was singing, 'Tell me, pretty maid', in a

Our last sett in Thursday's Tournament!!!
4th Oct.

comparable garment, to a rapturous audience in York. Have not confided this nonsense to anyone.

Last morning on the Esplanade Wednesday. 17th Oct. Harold's chair finished. Started for Waterloo by the 1.30. Our dear old Noggie accompanied me as far as Portsmouth & saw me safely started from there. Fog in London

Dear Harold Pope has finished the chair he has been making for Nannie. Much touched by his concern. It is a most exquisite piece of design, and will give Nannie many happy hours of pleasure. Major Brown and I took her out for her first airing in it this morning. She wrapped herself up in her fur-trimmed coat and veil with quite a skittish air, and we simply sped along the esplanade. Every few minutes, Nannie spied some old acquaintance with whom it was imperative she exchange words, and would signify her desire to stop with a peremptory stamp of her little foot on the floor of the chair. Fear the chair may not last long under such punishing treatment, but the outing was deemed a great success by all.

Started for London by the 1.30 pm. Tearful farewells to Lilian and Steakie. Lilian much concerned that I am so excited by the prospect of my trip. Explained it was only natural to wish to see the friends of one's youth. The Great G and Nannie loaded me with messages for friends and relations. Nannie popped a teapot, round which ran lettering, 'Ventnor from the Sea', into my Japanese basket and we were off. Noggie thoughtfully volunteered to take me as far as Portsmouth, and, with the assistance of some very helpful porters and a kind gentleman in the train who lavished periodicals on me, and told me a great deal about his life as a travelling salesman, I arrived safely in London.

London buried in fog. Went to Harrow for the day to see the Welsfords. Mr Welsford locked in combat with two wicked boys who had broken bounds and bought strong drink. Their pallor in Morning Prayers had given them away. Tried to cheer them — they looked so wretched — with the story of when Lilian and I had got quite tipsy on punch, but Mr Welsford hurried them into his study. Had lunch with all twenty-nine boys. They chattered like magpies. Afterwards, Alice took me all over the school. Beautiful views of London and much admired the Welsfords' house. Japanese embroideries hang beside the curtains, and there is some lovely Dutch marquetry.

Passed a most tiring day in London, going to the Italian Exhibition. The rooms were full to bursting. Finally found solace for my poor tired feet on a bench in the last room.

my most vivid impression of the Italian Exhibition

November 1888

The twin towers of York Minster loomed with gratifying solidity as the train came in. Felt waves of nostalgia, such as, I believe, Oxford scholars feel on returning to that town. Not that I was ever much of a scholar at Miss Kirby's.

Struck out boldly for Burton Terrace, and, to my delight, hardly had I arrived when Lily North came to call. So much to go over, so many friends' stories to hear. Dozens of the old girls have got married, I gathered. Lily says she has been a bridesmaid time out of number. The last time, she was forced to wear puce, which did not accord at all well with her golden hair. Went with her to visit Miss Charlotte, who seemed quite unchanged. Her fringe was still straggling into her eyes, and her beaded bag seemed in constant and imminent danger of collapse all the time she was talking to us. She and Miss Kirby are so devoted to the interests of their pupils past and present, it is quite touching. Two young girls sat with us throughout our tea, quite silent. Miss Charlotte informed me they were present for the benefit of my conversation. Wondered if my prattle deserved the attention.

Wandered out to revisit my old haunts. Walked out to see the fields of chicory. Such pretty blue flowers. Walking back, however, erred in my path and plunged into Hungate, by mistake.

The Daily Round, The Common Task

Our nightly lock-up round.

Had forgotten the miserable poverty of the area. An old Irish woman looked up from her clay pipe which she was sucking on a kerbstone and muttered something unintelligible but distinctly rude. A small boy by her side advanced and pulled at my skirt. Shook him off and fled. Quite distressed by the incident all evening. Resolved to do what I could to help. Lily mentioned a plan to alleviate the drunkenness in the area, setting up coffee stalls outside the public houses. Seems a wonderful idea.

Went with Lily on an architectural tour this morning. Strolled round the Gothic arches of St Mary's Abbey, and met two Americans, father and son, who are come here to find out their family history. Asked us if we knew anyone called Philpotts. Had to disappoint them. Old Mr Philpotts, a very courteous gentleman in spite of wearing odd yellow boots, asked if they could accompany us on to the Archbishop's Palace. Hesitated, but decided, as they were visitors from overseas, that it was our duty to welcome them to our shores, and could not be construed as fast. Young Mr Philpotts insisted on including us both in a sketch he made of the palace pilasters. Returned home, rather excited by this brush with the New World, but deemed it prudent not to mention it.

Called at Cliff Villa—Edith was out—and then at No. 17 Bootham. Such elegant Georgian houses. Never appreciated their beauty when I was a hoydenish schoolgirl. Miss Kirby led us in an impromptu concert. I sang 'Greeting' and some improvised duets with Lily. Spent the evening writing programmes for the grand dance.

Tonight was the occasion of the dance at Mansion House. Never seen it look so fine, banks of flowers ringing the hall and chandeliers ablaze with gas lights. I wore my new dress made by Mrs Gibbon, black satin trimmed with chenille and beads.

Lily wore a dark green dress she did not care for, as she confided to me. Nevertheless she had no shortage of partners. Having been so long out of the district, I found myself without a partner for a *valse* late in the evening, but I consoled myself, talking to Mrs Sydenham Walker who does not dance on account of her foot.

The Belle of the Ball.

Prince Albert Victor 'Eddie' was present, looking immensely smart. Most of the evening he spent in a smoking-room, but, as Charlie Cooper was whisking me round in the Gondolier *valse*, a Presence bore down on us and nearly trampled us underfoot. It was the Prince, sporting a tuxedo, which caused a great stir. All the other men in their swallow-tails suddenly looked quite drab.

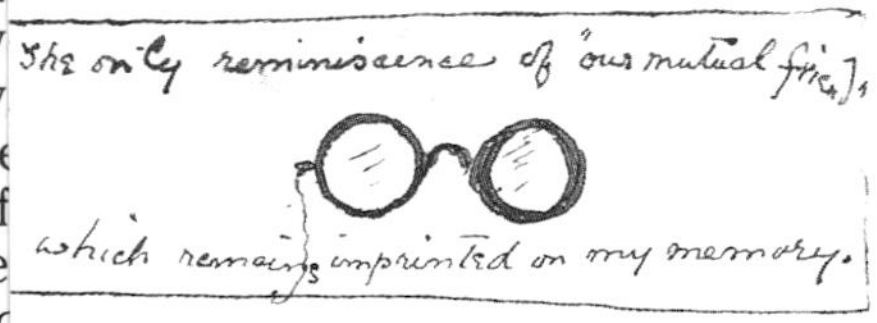

The only reminiscence of 'our mutual friend',
which remains imprinted on my memory.

Stayed at home till the late afternoon. Then spent the evening with Miss Charlotte. Very cosy. chatted over old days at Miss Kirby's, and Lily and I spent splendid hours recalling times past. Reminded her of the time we climbed onto the school roof and hung the Viper's new muffler as a flag from the chimney.

Went to St Martin-cum-Gregory. Always pleased to see my favourite stained glass window, a memorial by William Peckitt to two of his daughters who died young. Saw several of the old girls, including Bertha Stanhope who has married very well. She was wearing some very ornate filigree jewellery. Rather over-dressed for church, we all agreed, and she barely nodded to us, once the service was over. Swept away in a hansom cab, without so much as enquiring after the Great G and Nannie, who had always been very kind to her as a dull young girl.

Been to several lectures at the Museum, among them one on 'Pygmies'. Very interesting. Quite altered my view of the Congo. Such a vivid picture of events, I half expected to see small figures with blowpipes when I emerged onto the street. Went to another, on 'The Progress of Women'. Feel Steakie would have approved. Delivered by a very fiery lady, who gesticulated wildly with every point she made. Heard afterwards she is a canon's aunt who has long lived in America.

Mr Noble came to photograph us today, and after lunch we played tennis in the Drill Hall. Then I led an expedition up to the Retreat to see the Bakers. Dr Baker had to leave the tea-table suddenly, when a report came that one of the patients imagined his bed was covered in spiders and needed to be reassured on the point. He was causing havoc in the ward, upending beds to see if other patients were suffering from the same problem. Dr Baker was imperturbable as ever. Not by so much as a twitch of his moustaches did he allow us to notice his distress. Strangely, though, he kept twitching at his trousers, as though he had been infected by his patient's diseased imagination into thinking there were creatures where there were not.

Went to see Kate, our housemaid, in the hospital. She looked very peaky and hardly well enough to thank me for the flowers I brought her. Her mother, a thin, sad woman in black with protuberant teeth, was with her, so I did not stay long. Suggested she stay there till she felt fully recovered, but her mother looked quite put out and muttered she had a family to feed, and could not keep coming to look after an idle daughter. Feel Kate would have done better to stay at Burton Terrace, but Beatrice has a horror of infection.

Forgot Kate's woes, preparing the house for the dance. We had a fearful battle the day before it, attempting to shift all the furniture up and down the stairs. We tied up our hair with bandanas to avoid the penalty of shampooing twice in a week, and carried tables upstairs and chairs downstairs with great fervour. Lily introduced me to a new confectioner, whom we patronized extensively. Exhausted by the evening. Wrote out the last of the programmes and did Derby and Joan in the study. Dreamt vividly that a fire broke out during the second *valse*. Greatly relieved to awaken.

Buzzed about the house all day, arranging flowers and directing a multitude of tradesmen who arrived with various offerings. The raspberries for the meringues failed to arrive, to our general consternation, but Beatrice persuaded me no one would remark on it. Regret having boasted to Charlie Cooper of this treat in store.

The dance itself seemed quite an anti-climax after all the hard work we had put into it. Charlie Cooper did not arrive till halfway through the evening. He had been closeted with the organist at St Martin-cum-Gregory, and then dined with the Yorkshire Philosophical Society. Forgot his serious avocations long enough to twirl me in two *valses*, but felt his mind was on higher things. Dr Baker another distracted partner in the Lancers. Confided that one of the warders at the Retreat had been discovered, stealing money from the Benevolent Fund, by a patient. A rum state of affairs, as he expressed it.

Very pleasant day, after the dance. Set the house to rights, and then, in the evening, held a small impromptu concert with Lily for the family.

Went with Mrs Sydenham Walker to the Chrysanthemum Show. Very crowded. Could hardly see the plants for the hordes, but saw

December 1888

Long and troubled journey finally brought me to the parental home. Very sad to part with all the friends in York, but, speed e'er so well the coming year, we will all meet next year, as I told them all. Changed trains at London, and could not resist the opportunity to wander about on the station at Waterloo. The result was, my trunk went flying in one direction and my boxes in another, as I had neglected to inform the two porters who were helping me just where I was going. At last in Portsmouth, found to my delight, Lilian and Steakie had come to meet me. Had much to tell them. Steakie keenly interested by news of the lecture on 'The Progress of Women'. Lilian just a mite put out that I had not had time to write copiously to her.

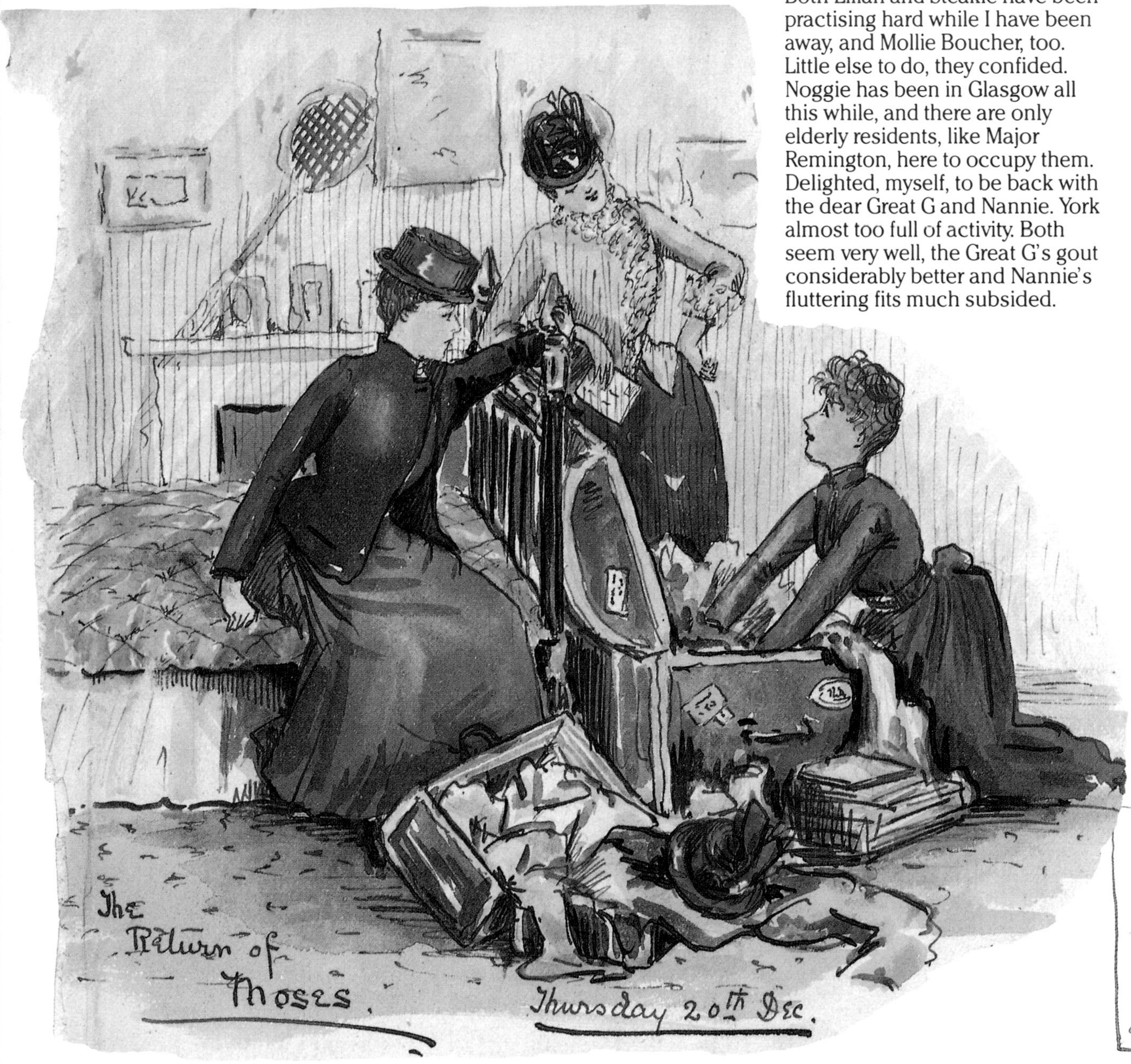
The Return of Moses.
Thursday 20th Dec.

Unpacked all day, and buzzed around, seeing friends. Had done most of my Christmas shopping in York. Bought very tasteful pictures of the Minster, which I plan to distribute when I have added a touch of colour with ivy leaves and holly berries. Could not think what to buy for Lilian, so have embroidered an apron which she can perhaps wear when dressing as a maid at concerts.

Both Lilian and Steakie have been practising hard while I have been away, and Mollie Boucher, too. Little else to do, they confided. Noggie has been in Glasgow all this while, and there are only elderly residents, like Major Remington, here to occupy them. Delighted, myself, to be back with the dear Great G and Nannie. York almost too full of activity. Both seem very well, the Great G's gout considerably better and Nannie's fluttering fits much subsided.

Christmas comes but once a year and Sandown is as full of bunting and carols and Christmas candles as any other point in England. Little Ruby Barnes is in a feverish state of excitement, as she has been promised by her parents a particularly desirable doll from Mr Redfern's emporium in Cowes. Collingbourne has yielded a little to my strenuous attempts to bring some of the Christmas message of peace and good cheer within its doors. Not easy, as the Great G objects to some of the more enterprising ideas I had for enlivening the hall. Nannie and I managed to effect the planting in the hall, however, of one of the first Christmas trees to be seen on the Island—following the example Prince Albert set. Not sure if we will continue the custom next year. It seems to shed a good many needles all over the carpet. Much admired, however. Ruby immediately petitioned Mr Barnes for one just the same.

Christmas Day. The Firm all went to Christchurch in the morning, and on Parade afterwards. Mrs Hatchet pecked me on the cheek, such was the excess of Christmas spirit about. Then the Meeres came with an invitation for New Year's Eve, and stayed to tea. Afterwards we played the new 'Old Maid'. Lilian won, and celebrated by coming back to Fernside with me for tea and a rubber of whist with the Great G and Nannie.

On Boxing Day, we strolled out along the esplanade in the morning, and found Mrs Shepherd basking in the sun. We borrowed her paper to read for a short time, so as to say it was possible to sit and read out of doors on Boxing Day. In the

a Reminiscence of Boxing Day.

ıfternoon, we had a rehearsal at he Bouchers', and then tea and games at the Meeres'. Helped Lilian with a few programmes in he evening.

The Hargroves had their ıfternoon dance in the Odd Fellows' Hall. Very nice to see all he winter faces.

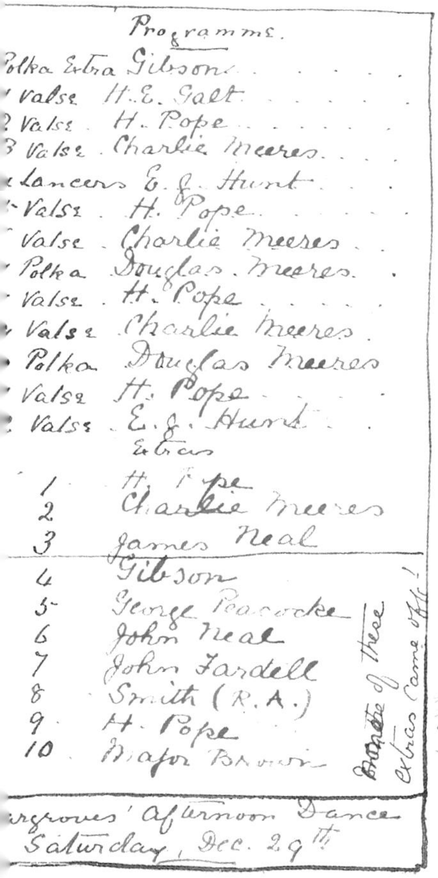

Programms.

Polka Extra Gibson
Valse H. E. Galt
2 Valse H. Pope
3 Valse Charlie Meeres
Lancers E. J. Hunt
Valse H. Pope
Valse Charlie Meeres
Polka Douglas Meeres
Valse H. Pope
Valse Charlie Meeres
Polka Douglas Meeres
Valse H. Pope
Valse E. J. Hunt
Extras
1 H. Pope
2 Charlie Meeres
3 James Neal
4 Gibson
5 George Peacocke
6 John Neal
7 John Fardell
8 Smith (R.A.)
9 H. Pope
10 Major Brown

None of these extras came off!

Hargroves' Afternoon Dance
Saturday, Dec. 29th

Went to Christchurch with The Firm in the morning, and then on Church Parade, after which we had a long and muddy constitutional with the Lamb. In the evening we went to Shanklin Church. Rather tired after all this church-going, but it has, on balance been a happy year. Ended off the annum, jumping over candles with Mollie and Steakie at the Bouchers.

Arrival of a Cat
Xmas card (from McDougal)
on Xmas Eve -

Dec. 31st
New Years Eve!
None of the candles blew out!!!

January 1889

The New Year dawns, and, with it, more tasks for the unwary. Helped to polish the floor of the Oddfellows' Hall this morning. Dear Lilian would have helped, only her back was still hurting after our vigorous exercise on New Year's Eve. Mrs Barnes very rightly suggested she rest till the dance, and Lilian seemed thankful to do so, if disappointed not to join in the fun. Happily, her back recovered wonderfully and she was able to dance with her usual verve with Noggie when jollities began. I danced one of the Extras with Harold Pope.

Finished making my White Moth dress for the Shanklin Fancy Dress Dance. Found the idea in an old book of fairy tales belonging to Ruby Barnes. The White Moth flitted about and promoted harmony wherever she settled. Thought, as I sewed my dress, of the numerous occasions where I might do the same. Went over to Collingbourne to see how Lilian and Steakie were faring with their costumes. Found Lilian, who is going as Starry Night, was in despair, not knowing where to find silver tissue with which to wrap her wand. We sauntered out and discovered, by a lucky chance, the milliner's in the High Street had just the thing, wrapped round the brim of a very ugly hat. We persuaded her she would not miss the ornament for a short space of time, and received permission to borrow it for the dance. Returned to Collingbourne to find Steakie was taking the wise precaution of boiling the eggs she planned to carry in her basket in her character of Red Riding Hood.

The most difficult part, when dressing as a White Moth, is preserving the proper ghostliness of appearance. To this end, I powdered my hair thoroughly and made a paste of flour and water, which I applied liberally to my face and arms. Found, when I reached the dance, that my partners were all rather disconcerted to find their coats and hands a touch besmeared by my mixture. Most of them laughed it off, but Charlie Meeres, who was wearing a new silk coat, was not amused.

Steakie quite stole the show as Red Riding Hood, even Harold Pope unbending so far as to seize the eggs from her basket and attempt to juggle them in the air. A sorry mess resulted, but, as it was past three in the morning, we were all too merry to care. I danced several *valses* with Harold Pope. Could see, out of the corner of my eye, that Mrs Pope was not best pleased, but, frankly, too entranced by Harold in his Windsor dress to care.

Rushed down to Turton's this morning to get the powder shampooed out of my hair. Thought with satisfaction, on the whole, of the night's doings. Walked with Lilian as far as

"The Firm" at the Shanklin Fancy Dress Dance
Friday. 4th Jan.

Shanklin fancy dress dance in evening. got home at 4.40 a.m.

Programme of Shanklin Fancy Dress
Friday. Jan. 4th

Eastern Dress	1	Valse	Dr. Freitas	Les Cloches de Corneville
Windsor Dress	2	Valse	H. Pope	With the Stream
R.E. Uniform	3	Lancers	Douglas Meeres	Lord of Lorne.
white coat & black shirt	4	Polka	Basil Peile	Jolly Blacksmiths
R.A. militia Uniform	5	Valse	Wilfrid Parker	Under the Stars
Barrister	6	Valse	Gibson	Elysium.
Windsor dress	7	Valse	H. Pope	Venezia
Neapolitan	8	Polka	F.W. Fisher.	A.B.C.
R.A. Uniform	9	Valse	Armstrong	Two Kisses
R.A. Uniform	10	Lancers	Smith	Caledonians
R.A. Uniform	Supper Dances i	Valse	Armstrong	Spirit of Love
Sandhurst	ii	Polka	G. Peacocke	Kutschke
D.D. gown	iii	Valse	Porter	Madame Favart.
Windsor dress	11	Valse	H. Pope	Old Love & the New
Indian dress	12	Polka	Arthur Welsford.	Outpost
Windsor dress	13	Valse	H. Pope	Fairie Voices
R.A. militia	14	Valse	Wilfrid Parker	Le Pitteria
R.A. uniform	15	Lancers	Smith	Dorothy
R.E. Uniform	16	Highland Schottische.	Douglas Meeres	
Eastern Dress	17	Galop.	Dr. Freitas.	Foxhunters
Barrister	18	Polka	Gibson	Old China
R.E. Uniform	19	Lancers	D. Meeres	Mikado
Windsor dress	20	Valse	H. Pope	True Love is sweet
Planter	21	Valse	Ernest Frere	Ma Mignonne
Neapolitan	22	Valse	F.W. Fishere.	Toujours et Encore

Extras.

Windsor dress	1.	H. Pope
R.A. Militia	2.	W. Nicholson.
Windsor Uniform	3.	Hales
D.D. gown	4.	Porter
	5.	Smith
Sir W. Raleigh	6.	Harrison

Yaverland. She confided to me that Wilfrid Parker had told her she made him think, in her Starry Night costume, of Byron's lines, 'She walks in beauty like the night'. Did not like to mention that I thought Lord Byron rather a poor poet. Would have preferred a quotation from Lord Tennyson, myself.

Went to Miss Hatchard's to have our fortunes told. Mine was most encouraging. I was advised to hope for small but substantial advances. Wondered whether I could possibly interpret this as meaning Harold Pope might invite me to tea at Appuldurcombe. Mollie Boucher had a fortune of such surprising brilliance—and we all saw her blush—that we wondered what secret she had been keeping from us.

Went with Lilian and Steakie to Christchurch in the morning, and did Church Parade. Windy day. Saw no one in particular whom we knew. Walked to Shanklin in the evening, and went to church there. Bea Frere looked particularly fine in a brocaded coat with fox fur. A rich aunt from America had sent it to her, she explained. The Firm thought it a trifle luxurious for kirk, but we kept silence and only admired.

Very busy helping Lilian and Steakie organize the new drawing-room at Collingbourne. All Sandown and most of Shanklin have gathered to suggest improvements. McDougal and Wilfrid Parker came to suggest we abandon our busy schemes to hang all the plates in one afternoon and, rather, have a lark and fix a booby-trap for the next visitor to enter. I demurred at first. It seemed a cruel trick to play. Wilfrid insisted, going to extraordinary lengths to achieve his effect. He borrowed the largest earthenware platter from the Collingbourne kitchen and balanced it on top of the door. Despite dreadful fears that Mrs Hatchet might appear and fall victim, it was Ernest Frere who passed under the fatal portal. He did not quite seem to see the joke.

Monday. 7th Jan. Here for tea Mrs. Meek, Rozzie, Steakie, Miss Hatchard, Miss Stainthorpe, McDougal, Mr. Smith & Mr. Armstrong.
Tuesday 8th Jan. Helped Rozzie to arrange the new Collingbourne drawing-room in morning. Had tea there in afternoon, & stayed dinner. "The Turkey".
From 'I. W. Guardian'
Miss Tomlinson, as "Ghost Moth," was delicately clad in short soft white dress, with folded wings of white swansdown, powdered hair, and antennae in her hair.
Miss Black-Barnes was delightfully adorned as "StarryNight;" she wore a short dress of dark blue satin, with overskirt and sleeves hanging from shoulders of silver tissue; her hair was powdered with diamond dust and surmounted with a silver star, with a star on her shoulder, and she carried a wand with star.
Miss E. Black-Barnes as "Red Riding Hood" was unique, the observed of all observers. She wore a skirt of royal blue cashmere, white nainsook pinafore with embroidery, red cloak with hood, and red shoes and stockings, and carried a basket containing honey pot, five eggs and a loaf of bread.
—Fixing the Booby Trap—
Wednesday 9th Jan.

We hung up plates and dishes at Collingbourne, assisted by McDougal and De Freitas, who are still laying waste the villages of the Island, while their ship gets new supplies at Portsmouth. McDougal very nobly helped us put together a new shelf and hang it. We gave him several cups of tea for his pains. Unaccountably, the paste pot tipped upside down while he was drinking his second cup, and deposited a thin layer of paste all round the rim. We did laugh.

Miss Hatchard came to tea at Collingbourne, while we were hiding from the snow and sleet, and taught us how to tell fortunes, then gave us a lesson on the guitar. We all greatly took to the instrument, and she has promised to return and give us some further instruction. Steakie was at first reluctant to join in, saying she preferred banjos, but she too yielded to persuasion.

The Great G has gout, and was in bed all day today. I took him volumes of Plato and Homer, and we solemnly read some of the more trenchant passages together. The Great G's nightcap slipped over his eye as he was mulling over a description of Odysseus in the toils of Scylla and Charybdis, and his ancient spectacles slipped down the side of the bed, which entailed a long hunt. Subsequently, we took to

playing whist, in the belief that it would create less agitation. Escaped over to Collingbourne for dinner.

Lilian and I went to Christchurch, and then did Church Parade. Met Colonel Jacob, who told us all about the Mrs Thompson row. Mrs Thompson was in Cowes, shopping at Redfern's, when she spied Mrs Hatchet at the millinery counter trying on the most hideous red hat, trimmed with osprey feathers. Mrs Thompson, so the story runs, could not forbear to cross the shop and admire Mrs Hatchet's headgear—unfortunately, with such a false smile that Mrs Hatchet was not deceived, and instantly tore it off. At which point, the shop assistant took umbrage. Ripples from this affair have been slowly spreading through Sandown all the week. Mrs Thompson's daughters gave Mrs Hatchet the cut direct in the greengrocer's on Tuesday.

Busy preparing for the play, *Naval Engagements*, in which we are to appear at the Town Hall. Major Brown has quite stolen the show at all the rehearsals as Dennis, the waiter in the Portsmouth inn where the action takes place. My part is the best I have had in theatricals for some time. Lilian was to have it, but, as she confided to me, she has an overwhelming dislike for calling attention to herself just at present. Wonder whether Noggie has intimated in some subtle way that he prefers her not to take part in theatricals. Had no idea that so much of an understanding existed between them. I play a young girl who entraps first an admiral, and then a lieutenant, into an engagement. Not sure I would not rather embrace Major Brown than Douglas Maclaren, who plays the lieutenant.

Distinctly pleased with my costume, anyway. Dainty buckled shoes and a draped bodice set off a quilted skirt, and I applied two patches of rouge to each cheek, which gave me quite a saucy air.

Mr Boucher and his orchestra received more applause than any of the actors, and were warmly praised in the *Isle of Wight Guardian*. Jessie Boucher's violin playing was singled out for praise, which made us all very happy, as she has been learning so short a time. We tried to persuade her to join the *corps dramatique*, when we all went down next day to Debenham's to be photographed, but shyness prevailed. Or else she did not wish to be seen making a guy of herself with us.

Went to Collingbourne, where Milly Hatchard gave Lilian and me a guitar lesson, Kate Hatchard gave Steakie a banjo lesson, and poor Mr Barnes tried to have a vestry meeting with Mr Mouton and Dr Neal in the dining-room. Met Shoggie in the morning, who suggested, as it was a lovely day, we walk to Bembridge Links in the afternoon. Started with every good intention, but only got as far as Dr Hunt's, where we found tea and a basket-chair only too tempting an alternative. Consoled ourselves for our rudeness to Shoggie with the thought that he could practise his strokes much better in our absence.

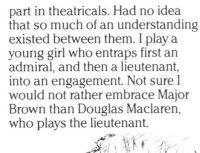

February 1889

Mrs Willan came over and, most flatteringly, implored me to act the part of 'Milkmaid' in her Amateur Theatricals. Delighted to oblige, though discovered afterwards that she had asked all the Boucher girls and the Welsfords first. Quite frightening, acting opposite Captain Willan. His moustache comes perilously near when he leans over to sing his refusal to marry me. He told me afterwards he thought I made a most delightful picture in my red petticoats, seated on my milking stool. Did not know what to say. Saw Mrs Willan's brows rise in disapproval.

Captain Willan paid me a visit unexpectedly, declaring he needed to practise his part for the Singing Tableau again. The Great G was in the library and came out with a most fearsome scowl, wanting to know what was going on. Tried to placate him, but the sight of an unknown man in the house sent him into an apoplectic rage. He kicked open the front door and suggested Captain Willan pass through it forthwith. Judge of my embarrassment.

Captain Willan sent a note, very neatly expressing his sorrow at having upset the Great G. The Great G mollified. The ban on appearing in the Tableau lifted. Off to the Primrose League Meeting. Sang 'Where are you going to, my pretty maid?' Encored. Feel it was more than half due to the primrose hat I wore. Lilian was kind enough to tell me it cast a most flattering light on my face. At one point, the brim flopped over one eye, so that I could scarcely see Captain Willan, let alone the audience, but Lilian assured me it only added to the effect.

Very cold and windy all this week. Lilian and Steakie and I have huddled at Collingbourne, entertaining ourselves with guitar lessons and practising duets. Went to Yaverland church for a change, and found a hurricane blowing when we emerged. Constitutionals on the sea wall have an extra spice when there is constant danger of being blown into the sea by gales.

Lilian ill in bed. Mrs Barnes blames the excessive number of walks we have taken in this uncertain weather. Took Lilian some quince jam, and read *Little Lord Fauntleroy* to her, which proved a very cosy treat. Both of us agreed that, were we ever to have a son, Cedric would be a prime favourite for one of his names. Discussed whether a Little Lord Fauntleroy suit of blac

A spectacle which the Station Rd. is often treated to.

elvet might not suit some of the
sland children. Mrs Barnes,
vhen appealed to, was frankly
ampening, and said she thought
ersey much more suitable as
material.

Valked to Shanklin in the
fternoon. Saw a very strange
gure on the step of the Crab Inn,
gentleman in a Norfolk jacket
nd knickerbockers, with bicycle
ropped against the wall, and
ketching book in hand. Lilian
nd I both sneaked a look at his
ork, and later privately agreed
hat we thought it hardly worth
is while progressing further.

is composition was quite unlike
e neat sketches of the Crab Inn
nd the cottages which we are
ccustomed to see. It was more
ke those strange paintings of
r Turner's, which some of the
ore advanced thinkers in our
ketching Club affect to admire.
ull of sound and fury, Signifying
othing', to my mind. So bitterly
old, and we were so miserable
n the way back, we felt 'druv' to
ail a coal-cart, and ask for a lift
ome. As we could not agree
hich of us was to speak, we let
e opportunity drift away.
erhaps it was as well. The cart
rned round and went off
Ventnor.

r Barnes is my Valentine this
ar. I presented him with a card,
overed in pressed violets, with
e injunction that he should give
e anything I wanted all year. He
d not seem to rate this treat as
gh as he might, and retreated
to his library, muttering that he
d vestry service to think of.

lled at Godshill Park, rather
ped we might see Harold Pope,
Appuldurcombe is so close by.
d to run for the train at both
ds, and, as my heel had come
at the park gates, only just
ade it to the train. The whole
lage came out to cheer our last
n up the station hill.

d a very droll private rehearsal
h Mr Fisher of our parts for the
llans' Tableaux. Fear the
llans may not see the joke, but
found we could make our
bleau screamingly funny.

March 1889

Lilian and I looked in at the Town Hall to see the rehearsal of the Mad Tea Party. Nothing but theatricals all this year. Feel we are all becoming quite accomplished actors. Mr Fisher and I both enjoyed ourselves immensely in the Primrose League play, *Why Women Weep*. I wore white muslin as the bride. A nasty accident nearly befell me, when Mr Fisher toasted the play in punch, and his glass tipped over me. Happily, Mrs Willan produced some violet-scented soap, and the offending patch was soon wiped clean. An aroma of violets wafted in my wake all day. Captain Willan did not hesitate, of course, to seize the opportunity to read poor Mr Fisher a lecture on the evils of strong drink.

March 4th Monday
waiting for the cue to go on.

Accompanied Lilian over to Shanklin with a Brobdingnagian parcel. We quarrelled all the way about who should carry it, and nearly fell over the cliff at one point in our efforts to snatch it one from the other.
Met Mrs Hatchet on our return, who tried to inveigle us into her house for a cup of tea, but, thankfully, we could make the decent excuse that we had to practise our duets for the Concert.

Lovely day. Got up an expedition with Maclaren and The Bud to go over to Ryde. Set out in fine fettle, all three of us in our veils and the faithful boa as ever at the ready. Maclaren and The Bud were not amused by our dilatoriness, when it came to catching the electric railway back along the pier. They failed to understand that ladies walk at a somewhat slowe pace than gentlemen.

Had a quiet evening at home. Serenaded Deborah, the cat, by the fire, till late into the evening, the Great G and Nannie having gone to bed early.

Up early, and over to Appuldurcombe for tennis. Tremendous fun. Lilian and I vanquished Jessie and Mollie Boucher in three sets, to our delight. Harold Pope was, as eve a perfect host and we had delicious lemonade and cakes. The Bud, who had broken his ankle and so couldn't play, relieved his feelings of boredom by throwing some cakes at us. I caught Mrs Pope's eye, and blushed for his want of manners. Thankfully, the party broke up before further arguments could develop.

Thursday. 7th March
Deborah does not approve of being "Serenaded" with "Thy Face" &c.

Started a bad cold and a sore throat, and stayed in bed for three days in a row. Much cheered by dear Lilian, who brought over her work each day uncomplainingly. We read together, at my request, a good deal of Lord Tennyson's Works. Wicked Steakie sent over some poems by some young female poet, writing that she was unable to come personally, as she was busy attempting some verse herself. Much impressed, only Lilian says there is nothing romantic about the pieces she has so far seen.

Lilian has gone to stay with Lucy Gates. Begged her to consider that the Gates children are known for their rowdiness, and may well upset her delicate nerves. She would not be moved. Consented to send me a letter. Feel awfully miserable without her. Cheered myself up with a brisk walk along the sea wall.

Monday 18th March
"A curious kind of treat"

Annie has been looking very strained for some time. Came to me this morning to confide that her legs had fallen from under her, as she phrased it, this morning when she was boiling water for the Great G's tea. Advised her to go straight to bed, and donned her apron myself. Practised a new tune while I washed all the dishes. At a loss to know what to give the Great G and Nannie for dinner, in Annie's absence. Consulted a great number of recipe books, none of which seemed to propose anything I felt I could possibly make. Spent a great many hours making castle puddings. Then found the Great G had had a profound hatred of them from childhood.

Tuesday. March 26th
Practical application of "The Oiled Feather"

Mollie gave me an Ambulance Bandaging Interview in the afternoon. Looking forward to the Ambulance Levee at the Mainwarings'. Beginning to know the different forms of tourniquet.

Came home and found all the chairs squeaked most dreadfully. Put on my apron and out with the machine oil young Waley had given me before he left for Australia. Thought tenderly of him as I oiled all the castors.

April 1889

Cards under difficulties.
Saturday. March 30th

The Great G retired to his bed tonight with an unexplained feve Nannie and I were very anxious, and brought him tisanes and warm drinks, but nothing seeme to assuage his ills. In desperatior I suggested we played at cards, and this seemed to please. We played by the light of a candl till the candle guttered and our eye grew dim. As the Great G won, he nodded off to sleep quite happily Nannie, as ever forbearing, did not point out, as she might have done, that the Great G had achieved his win more by lookin at our cards than by paying attention to his own.

Mrs. Meek
Ethel Hargrove
Mabel Jacob
Alice
Maud } Neal
Mary
Sleakie
Mollie
" Moses
Colonel Jacob
Charlie Meeres
D. McLaren
The Bud.

The exigencies of the road are not conducive to conversation

Pride goes before a fall!

Our Guide.

Waiting for tea

The "13th" had to share the window seat with the umbrellas!

Walking Expedition to S. Catherine's Light House
Friday. April 5th

Went on a marvellous walking expedition to St Catherine's Lighthouse. Alice, Maud and Mary Neal all looked very fetching with new boas — fit to rival mine — and new umbrellas. We were a very large party, only lacking Lilian for a full complement. Steakie and I had the greatest of fun, teasing Charlie Meeres. He suddenly declared his greatest ambition was to be a lighthouse keeper. Our guide, who took us over the lighthouse, was not encouraging, being much more intent on showing us the intricacies of the foghorn. It boomed out behind us quite frighteningly at one point.

Quite a dull week. Read fairy tales to Ruby Barnes and went for a walk on the sea wall with Steakie. Conversed at length about whether Noggie was really the right beau for Lilian. Went up to the Yaverland Road together on purpose to see Shoggie perform on the bicycle. He fell off twice, much to his discomfiture, but succeeded in riding with no hands down a stretch of road, which we all applauded.

To my great delight, Lilian returned tonight. She recounted o us all the trials and tribulations of staying with the Gates family. Little Albert Gates she announced o be a sweet boy, to whom she ead a great many fairy ales — though he did have a dreadful habit of pulling at the book with sticky hands. Victoria ane, however, she could not abide at any price. The child was always asking Lilian to give her a ibbon or show her how to thread a needle when Lilian was busy alking to Lucy.

Now Lilian is back, Sandown eems an altered place. We are busy organizing great walking parties and getting up dances. Took a table down to the Oddfellows' Hall, one being eeded for the ensuing dance. As usual, when bent on an errand of mercy, met Mrs Hatchet, who sked us darkly whether we had ecided to dismantle our arents' homes for good. Delightful dance. Harold Pope came over from Appuldurcombe and danced with me three times.

Went on a walking party to Shanklin on the beach this afternoon. We played hop-scotch and blind pigs on the sands. Shoggie distinguished himself by falling into the water on several occasions during the hop-scotch We went to the Crab Inn for tea, which was quite delightful, with scones and an enticing selection of sandwiches.

Mrs Barnes told me today that she thought of me quite as an extra daughter, which made me feel very happy. The fact that this was inspired by my having dined for the third successive day at Collingbourne in no way diminished the pleasure I felt at the compliment.

Lilian, Steakie and I all very keen to improve our tennis this spring. Played on Harry Maund's new court. Terribly pleased when Harry admired my new costume. Took in an old outfit of Lilian's and added little white bunches of flowers all round the hem. Harry said I reminded him of a narcissus.

Heard from Mrs Boucher that all the spring bulbs she planted have been eaten by old Mr Jenkins's donkey. Mr Boucher is threatening to shoot the donkey, and everyone is in the most tremendous stew about it. I suggested Mr Boucher buy a muzzle and offer it to Mr Jenkins, to prevent incidents of this kind happening again.

May 1889

Lilian, Steakie and I all went over to Ventnor for the dance at Hambrugh Hall, which proved the greatest success. The Bud, looking very smart in a new coat, was our escort, and did not fail to let us down, as usual. The carriage he ordered did not turn up till past four o'clock. We were all very anxious, and I feared that the Great G would not allow the expedition to take place. Nannie, however, provided her usual calming words of wisdom, and, come half-past four, the carriage arrived. We bundled ourselves up with rugs and shawls, and had a very merry drive over. The Bud, with great good sense, suggested we walk up the hills to save the horse. Poor old nag, it did not seem capable of much more than carrying us over to Ventnor. Very worried, when we arrived, whether it would manage the return journey, but my fears proved groundless. We danced till 2 am, and then, on our return all went into Collingbourne to have a chat. Lilian wanted us to play cards, but Mr Barnes, coming down in a nightcap and with a pained expression, put a stop to that. Finally crossed the road home at 4 am.

walking up the hills to save the horse

FELLOWS OF THE ROYAL SOCIETY.
Out of about eighty candidates, the following fifteen were selected by the Council yesterday afternoon for the Fellowship of the Royal Society:—Mr. J. Aitken, Dr. E. Ballard, Mr. A. B. Basset, Mr. H. T. Brown, Mr. L. Clark, Professor D. D. Cunningham, Mr. L. Fletcher, Mr. W. B. Hemsley, Mr. C. T. Hudson, Professor M'Kenny Hughes, Mr. E. B. Poulton, Professor W. J. Sollas, Mr. C. Todd, Mr. H. Tomlinson, and Professor G. F. Yeo.

Very tired this morning. Went out for a short walk on the esplanade, and then washed all the china in the drawing-room. Have tried to interest Nannie in the idea of buying some china from Italy called majolica. The Welsfords in Harrow had some beautiful examples. Sadly, Nannie seems quite content with the old gold and white plates, a present from St Peter's School on the Great G's retirement. She objects to the majolica as being foreign, even though I pointed out it was made by Mr Minton.

Walked over to Bembridge. Hot day, and our umbrellas more in need as walking sticks than as protection against the rain. The Bud was, as ever, the leader of the expedition. His long legs made nothing of the hills. I came a poor fifth, and Lilian laughed at me for not having my Island legs, even after six years of living here.

Sunday. 5th May
We make a call at Bembridge

Spent the day, very peacefully, making daisy chains for Ruby Barnes, while Lilian and Steakie played tennis on Harry Maund's court. Ruby recited to me nursery rhymes till they rang in my ears. She has grown up so fast this past year, she makes a very agreeable companion.

Lilian and Steakie, spurred on by Mr Barnes, have recently been taking the Coal and Clothing Club. I offered to help them, but they prefer to manage it alone. They told me there could be dreadful quarrels, such as when Mrs Jones and Mrs Crichton were in dispute over a jacket which would fit both little Jones and little Crichton. Lilian, very considerately, said she did not think I had the firmness necessary to deal with such troubles. Took Ruby down to the sands while they were thus engaged. Built castles and cakes and stables in the sand for her. Found I enjoyed the experience almost as much as she did. A wicked dog ran straight through my finest creation, a row of stables, but we rebuilt it without any tears from Ruby. She is a good child.

Emmie arrived by the seven o'clock train, to our delight. She has been very ill and has gone quite blind, so we were all concerned that she should have good rest on the Island. So nice to see her rosy face, though why she wears those old-fashioned bonnets when she is not a day beyond fifty I do not know.

Monday 6th May.
May 7th Wednesday
we are divided on one point only —
My husband imagines that The Greek bun is his style! — while I fix my hopes on a Cadogan.

preparatory to rejoining his regiment and he could not allow that carrying a bucket and spade accorded well with his dignity.

Tennis rather hampered by there being no nets without holes anywhere on the Island, as it seemed to us. Certainly, the Frere and Boucher nets badly needed rebinding. Accordingly, we set to and spent the morning binding one for the Freres, then felt too exhausted to do more. The Island laziness, which tourists always remark on, has been afflicting us badly this summer.

Her illness does not seem to have softened her strict temper. She lectured me, as usual, on the recklessness of my ways, and suggested I went to kirk a good deal more often. Remonstrated that I went twice each Sunday, as I was. To appease her, I read Renan's *Life of Jesus* aloud for what seemed like hours.

The Bud was deeply embarrassed when we persuaded him to come down with us and Ruby to the sands. He was in his uniform,

June 1889

None of the men being very enthusiastic to sample the delights of the great outdoors, we had a Ladies' Picnic in the Landslip. Mollie Boucher brought a teapot which leaked through the spout, so we were not very adequately served. The Neal girls looked on with a most superior air from a vantage point high on a rock, while we endeavoured to staunch the flow. It was so cold, that, after only an hour or so, we retreated back to Sandown.

Major Brown and I played tennis against Frank Barnes, just back from America, and Lilian. Frank looks immensely tanned and fit, and could talk of little else than a lovely girl he had met in Canada called 'Downie'. He showed us all her picture—which he had had specially engraved at considerable expense. Mrs Barnes, romantic soul, is in raptures, and shows the picture to all who come to Collingbourne with as proud an expression as if Downie were her daughter-in-law already.

Thursday June 6th
awful result of sheltering under Frank's roof.

A horrid encounter with a winged beastie in my bedroom caused me the greatest of trouble. I tried to dislodge it from the various positions it took up, with newspapers, umbrellas, and, finally, by standing in the middle of the room and waving my arms at it. Moths I abhor. Slept very badly, as a result, and dreamt at one point that an enormous moth was covering my face with its furry legs.

Went to the Militia Dance in the Town Hall. Harold Pope has gone to London on business, so I danced a good deal with Frank Barnes. Dear Frank, for all his good heart, he has the elegance of an elephant. Everyone looked

Saturday. June 15th
one of The advantages of having the Club-Courts so close together

very gay in their uniforms, but the best part of the evening was when Lilian and Steakie and I all found ourselves without partners, and escaped up to the gallery to watch the dancers from on high.

Steakie has gone off to Weymouth to pay a visit to her friend, Mabel Partridge, who has some very advanced notions on the role of Woman. Lilian and I both tried to dissuade her from going. Felt it might well encourage the very strange notions which Steakie has recently been indulging in. She was obdurate. We all went down to see her off—Lilian, Frank, Charlie Meeres and Charlie Sinclair. I had made a little cake, and adorned it with festive pink ribbons. I added a card which I had painted, with the motto, 'Speed you well'. Steakie seemed in raptures, and placed the card on the little table in her compartment, saying she was sure it would bring her luck. She looked very fetching, in a new hat trimmed with flowing maroon ribbons.

Lilian and I dined quietly at Collingbourne together, as Mr and Mrs Barnes were out at a Glee Club. Lilian seemed strangely excited. Felt it was rather heartless in her, considering Steakie had gone off to what might prove her doom. Only discovered this morning the reason for Lilian's agitation. Noggie has come back from Florida.

Noggie and Shoggie escorted us over to the cricket match—Shanklin against Appuldurcombe, today, Whit Monday. Very cold day. Nothing could prevail on me to attend another match this season. Noggie was in very fine form, and gave us dazzling descriptions of the climate and the fruit trees of Florida. We were so entranced, we quite failed to take note of the cricket ball which winged its way towards us after a heroic stroke by Wilfred Parker. Fortunately, Noggie, with eyes sharpened by the Atlantic wave, caught the ball with a deft lunge to the right. We gave thanks to him for preserving our hats from assault.

Shoggie, always with one eye on the needs of the stomach, suggested we all repair to Gray's for tea. A very sensible idea, as we had been driven to shelter behind the pavilion in the end, where we could see none of the match. The cold and draughtiness having proved unendurable. To complete our happiness, as we came home, the sea-fog resolved itself into a fine but penetrating rain.

Great fun today. Moie came round with an invitation to join her on a paddling party this evening. Her two dogs got inextricably tangled up with Nannie's knitting, bringing about the collapse of a jersey intended for Beatrice's little boy. Poor little Nannie was in tears. Tried to explain that dogs will be dogs, and that it was simply a case of high spirits. Feel she was not very much comforted. Very enjoyable paddling party. We splashed by the light of the moon till long after the water grew cold about our feet.

It was so cold & draughty at the Cricket match that we were obliged to shelter behind the Pavilion where we could see nothing.

2 and were finally driven to getting tea at Gray's

(1) I become suddenly aware of a "Presence" in the room –
(2) Efforts to dislodge the enemy by fanning it out of the room with a "Pictorial" only result in a narrow escape from total darkness
LADIES PICTORIAL
(3rd) The creature having "settled" after an exciting chase of 3/4 hours, I find a "husband-beater" very useful for eviction purposes.

Wore my new hat with cherries glued round the brim to an afternoon dance and tennis at Haslar. Weighed in heavily for strawberries and cream afterwards. Uncle Ward was most attentive, fresh from his ship.

Had a most enchanting day. Noggie and Lilian thought up the plan of taking our banjos down to Mrs Malden's and serenading her. She lost her husband three years ago, and, ever since, has lived in retirement. However, Noggie caught sight of her buying some jet baubles in Fenton's Millinery Department, so decided there was hope that she was thinking of relaxing her mourning. A tuneful serenade, he thought, might be just the thing to cheer her on her way.

Accordingly, The Firm, Uncle Ward, Noggie, Shoggie, Frank Barnes, Charlie Meeres and The Charmer all set out with missionary zeal. As luck would have it, when we arrived, we found that Mrs Malden was indeed relaxing her mourning and had gone off to Appuldurcombe to take tea with Mrs Pope. Felt more than half inclined to follow her there. Such a lovely house, and Harold Pope such a worthy heir to the property. Serenaded the maid, instead, who had given us the news, so as not to have made the journey for nothing. Rewarded with a shower of pennies, and had lovely ices at Mr Fountain's tea shop, in consequence.

Uncle Ward, that maritime soul, had been looking yearningly out to sea throughout our spell in the tea shop, and proposed suddenly that we should all take advantage of the glorious summer breezes and go for a sail on the sea. Shoggie, cautious as ever, insisted we return to our respective homes and delve out the Chinese lanterns we used for our Peking Picnic last year. The Great G unfortunately appeared as I was rooting around in the attic for my lantern.

Friday. June 21st. Afternoon dance & Tennis at Haslar. We weighed in heavily for strawberries & cream, & had a fairly good time. Home at 8 p.m.

Haslar Programme. June 21

1	Valse	Ernest Frere	3.30 p.m.
2	Valse	(ate strawberries with Roggie & Bea Frere)	3.45
3	Valse	Ernest Frere	4
4	Polka	De Freitas	4.15
5	Valse	Welch (fat man) (like Capt. Handley)	4.30
6	Valse	Ernest Frere (walked outside & saw Mrs Lilley)	4.45
7	Valse	(more straw berries & cream with Roggie)	5
8	Lancers		5.15
9	Valse	E. Powell	5.30
10	Valse	Ernest Frere	5.45
11	Polka	Bidwell	6
12	Valse	De Freitas	6.15 went home
13	Valse	E. Powell	6.30
14	Valse		6.45

10th extra Thring

I did not think he would object to the proposed expedition, but, as events turned out, he had been worried by hearing my scurrying footsteps overhead into thinking there was a mouse in the house, a thing he abhors. Accordingly, he made strenuous efforts to ban me from going on my junket—out of sheer bad temper, it seemed to me. But dear Nannie came out in her cap, and shed sweet reason all about. I rushed to join the others.

We rowed energetically by the light of the lanterns and saw quite a few friends bobbing about like ourselves in other crafts. Noggie was quite determined to salute a dim figure in a rowing boat close by, whom he declared he recognized to be Alice Welsford. Lilian had to restrain him from leaping into the ocean wave and swimming across to discover if it were really she. When the men's vigour failed them, they brought us back to shore and we sang our way back along the Prom and up the High Street, quite blown to bits with the refreshing sea air.

Went to see Frank Barnes off on his journey to New Brunswick. Dear little Downie is anxiously awaiting him, all her family eager to see her chosen one. Mrs Barnes has sent photographs, and in one of them she was pleased to include me. M.T. goes to New Brunswick.

Picked a bouquet of wild flowers to mark the occasion of Frank's departure by the 8.30 am train. A little difficulty arose, as the flowers were growing at the back of Mrs Hatchet's garden and, as I was picking them, she suddenly emerged from her conservatory. She declared herself passionately fond of the weeds I was clutching over the fence. Stuff and nonsense, I thought to myself, but I bore off my bouquet with due apologies. Unfortunately, it took so long, tying a velvet ribbon round the stalks, that, by the time I arrived at the station, the train was pulling out and so Frank never received his token. I gave it to dear Mr Porteus, the station master, instead. He looked quite perplexed by the gift.

(No 2) On the sea, June 28th

(No 3) June 28th. High Street. Escorting Moie home.

"Off by the morning train
Across the raging main
To do the grand in a distant land
Ten thousand miles away"
June 29th Saturday
Exciting scene at the Station. 8.30 a.m.

August 1889

Annie started off today for her annual holiday. Gave her a bunch of pressed violets to ward off the dreadful odours in the train. Dined at Major Remington's to meet his niece, a vicar's daughter from Brampton. Discussed the rival attractions of Sandown and Shanklin, to both of which she is new. Strange to say, she did not seem very impressed by either, and said she would be glad to get back to Cumberland. Major Remington was lighting his pipe, and affected not to, or perhaps truly did not, hear.

Lunched on board the *Immortalité*. Uncle Ward a very charming host. Saw the German Emperor and the Squadron come through the Solent, a very stirring sight. All the sailors on the *Immortalité* lined up and saluted, and, in my enthusiasm, I threw my boater in the air. Uncle Ward looked a trifle bemused by this, especially as he had to catch the boater before it flew overboard.

A hurricane blew all day today. Sea-fog and rain whirled about us as we set off, in mackintoshes and galoshes, for the Naval Review at Stokes Bay. Had a robust lunch, with roast beef and a galantine of chicken, before we discovered the Naval Review had been postponed. Went round the Fleet in a steam-launch, instead, which was the greatest of fun. I found a dry, warm and comfortable seat on the boiler with the chimney as a back. Wilfrid Parker, who accompanied

R.E. Pier Stokes Bay
Waiting for lunch, & for the rain to clear off. Aug. 3rd

We found the most comfortable seat was The boiler, with The chimney as a back.

Beg yer parding Miss, but woul
you come out of that — we can't
get no air down below here.

us on the expedition, sat with me and protected me with an umbrella from the worst of the rain. Immensely enjoyable day, and a great treat to see our brave sailors in such spirits.

Had a telegram to say the parents were on their way home. Thought up a surprise with which to welcome them back. Painted a banner with the words, 'Welcome Home', and decked it all about with rosebuds. Added some sunflowers and convolvulus. Felt it made quite a pretty picture. The Great G professed himself charmed with it.

The Hatchards invited us all to a Coaching Picnic at Carisbrooke castle. Lilian and I, knowing these picnics of old, took with us our darning and, as soon as the festivities were over, we took out our stockings and holed up in a room in the Castle. Dougie Maclaren and Douglas Meeres watched us with amusement. Told they were expected to wander about the castle grounds, they soon found their way to the warmth of our retreat. When the time came to depart, Mrs Hatchard sent out emissaries to find us, and great was young Jimmy Hatchard's surprise when he discovered us at our mending.

Colonel Berkeley is here on a holiday. Brought me news of his son, Bruce, whom I have not seen since his visit last year. Colonel Berkeley such a distinguished man. He still seems to feel the death of his wife very badly. Though Lilian and I tried by every means we knew to cheer him, giving him recitals on the banjo and any amount of strumming on the guitar, his face seemed set in an impenetrable gloom. He is such a very fine looking man, it seems a great shame. We took him to the children's party at the Oddfellows' Hall. Major Brown and Colonel Jacob came to help, too. Lilian and I dressed up as servants and helped to wait. It was the greatest of fun, and two dances were played at the end for our special benefit.

Lilian and I have invited Colonel Berkeley to share with us in a picnic at Whitecliff Bay. Wondered if our invitation was quite proper, but Lilian quelled my doubts. Have not told Nannie or the Great G of the third party in our expedition. Could not sleep last night for worrying. Would a soldier of Colonel Berkeley's distinction really care to bivouac on the downs with us? Should I pilfer a bottle of wine from the cellar to add cheer to the occasion? What should I wear?

It all passed off relatively well. Colonel Berkeley does have the most distinguished manners. He refused to take the last Scotch egg. Possibly he saw that Lilian was eyeing it hungrily. And, thank heavens, he brought his own bottle of stout. As we had forgotten the sandwiches, we were suitably grateful when, on our return to Sandown, the Colonel bought us all tea and scrumptious scones at Agatha's tea rooms. Such a lively sense of humour. He said he had had more to eat when on duty in the Kashmir hills. Think he was joking. He bought us both boxes of chocolates to end a perfect day.

A remedy against boredom.
Having been told by our hostess that after lunch we should be expected to wander about the ruins in pairs — Rozzie & I agreed to pair off by ourselves, find a secluded spot & darn our stockings. Our plan was rather spoilt by the ~~train~~ rain.
The Hatchard's Coaching pic-nic to Carisbrooke Wednesday. Aug. 14th

September 1889

Noggie and Lilian and I all had a set of tennis with Major Brown. It went as well as could be expected, considering the poor Major had broken his ankle some few weeks before and could hardly move across the court. Noggie made up for his opponent's poor performance with some wonderful balletic leaps across the court. Lilian was left standing as he issued forth with great empressement. At one point, we thought he might leap the net, such was his excitement.

Went to a cricketing lunch, where the wasps were out in force. Lilian and I almost dropped our scones and cups of tea as they buzzed about us. Douglas Meeres, who had been playing, came over to remonstrate with us for interrupting his game. He was out, leg before wicket, as he had been put off by seeing our skirts and sashes fluttering in the breeze. Returned to the trestle table and sat demurely through the rest of the day's proceedings.

The Mysterious Musicians came to Sandown and gave a concert. We all applauded wholeheartedly and gave of our best when they ended. They looked very striking in their uniforms of sou'westers and mackintoshes. Lilian and I approached them afterwards to see if they would consider appearing at a concert we plan giving at Collingbourne to mark Lilian's birthday. Unfortunately, they were busy with engagements all through the summer, and could not oblige.

Tuesday. Sept. 3rd. Shared Lunch & wasps with the Cricketers.

Went to call at Appuldurcombe. A dog came out and flew at me, but with my husband-beater I warded it off. Lilian and Steakie cowered craven behind the colonnades. I would have none of this cowardice, and ventured out to conciliate it.

Lily Berkeley has come to join her father. She has entered into Island life with alacrity, and displays sparkling form. Her hair is like silk, very long, and she wears it in two braids wrapped around her head. Colonel Berkeley, to

celebrate her arrival, took us all to Dore's, and treated us to ices in the morning. In the afternoon, he presented us both with a large box of chocolates.

Played tennis with Major Brown and Mr Kingsmill and Lily Berkeley. The weather much cooler. We all played with great vigour. Almost the end of the season for our summer visitors. The Berkeleys go off tomorrow, as does Alice Wolford. Sad to see them go. The Island will be the poorer for their parting.

Madame Erazuriz is here, looking splendid in furs and boas. She is of foreign extraction, which makes it all the more exciting for us residents. We are not accustomed to seeing ladies of fashion draped about with exotic lynxes. She acquired a taste for the Island when she came with her husband, a musician, in the seventies. She is still accustomed to come here every year. She lodges at the Seaview Hotel, and keeps the hotel staff in a perpetual anxiety. Her demands are so overreaching, they never know from one moment to the next what she will ask for. She has decided pretensions in the direction of music and sits at concerts, humming along to the tunes. The musical director of the Assembly Rooms at one point had to approach her and ask her to refrain from waving her *lorgnette* at the conductor when she felt the tempo was a little too fast.

Went to a wonderful dance at Westfield. I sat in a chair under a palm after an enchanting moonlit walk—although it was somewhat damp underfoot. Danced a great deal with Harold Pope, always a pleasure. He complimented me on my dancing. Feel those lessons long ago at Miss Palmer's in York, tiresome though they were, may pay dividends.

Lilian and Steakie and I all retired to Fernside where we sat by the fire. I entertained them with the breakdown which I had learnt for my banjo. They both yawned their way through the performance, so I left off. Wrote my diary till late into the night to make up for the disappointments of the day.

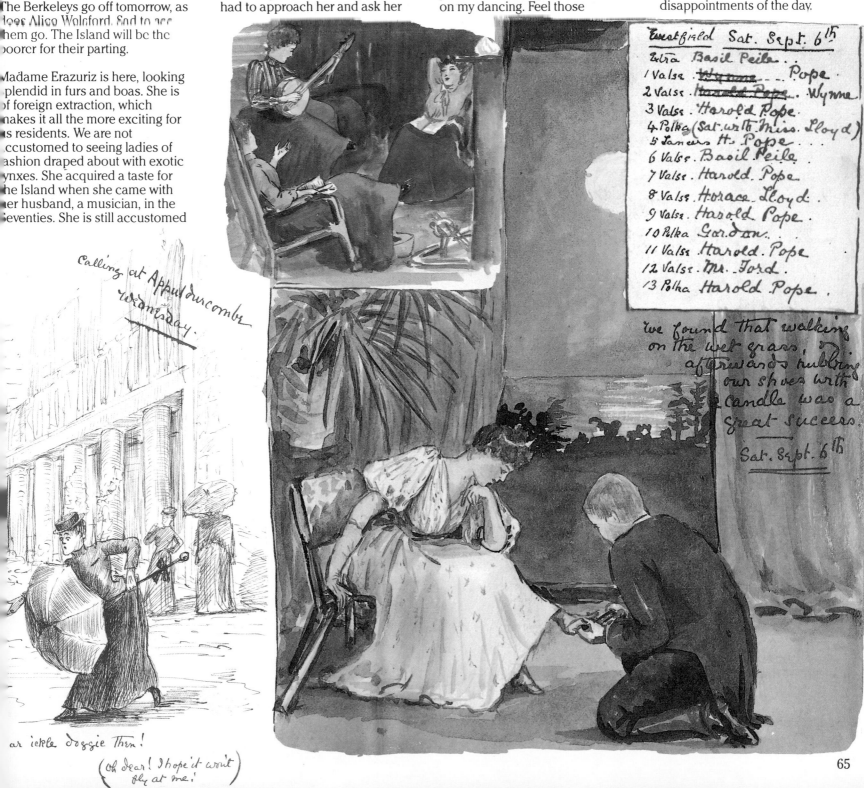

October 1889

Taught Madame Erazuriz to play tennis on the Freres' court at Shanklin. She is keen to play one game at the Club before the season ends in a few days' time. She proved an apt pupil and distinguished herself by hitting the ball over the net at least three times out of sixteen attempts. There was one embarrassing moment, though. The large white hat she insists on wearing blew off in the excitement of a rally. As she stooped to pick it up, I saw her luxuriant dark brown hair, coiffed in a chignon, suddenly fall from her head and lie like a stranded velvet cap on the tennis court. Madame Erazuriz was bald as a coot.

Thank heavens Mr Frere was not watching. With the greatest aplomb, Madame simply picked up the wig and replaced it on her head, topping the whole with her hat. Neither of us referred to this incident either then or later. 'Thirty love to you, was it not?' she asked, and we continued the game. Have not told even Lilian of my embarrassing discovery. Madame Erazuriz has now left Sandown, so there is no point. Especially as, before she left, she insisted on buying us each a photograph frame in the Arcade.

Felt very stupid all day. Made a night-dress case. Germany has fallen through. None of our parents are prepared to let us go. Lilian and I had set our hearts on it. We had dreams of wandering, alpenstocks in hand, over the Black Forest. Regret having spent three shillings on a German phrase book.

Made Scotch shortcake today in the Collingbourne Kitchen. Lilian and I both found the experience deeply gratifying, rolling our fingers round in the flour and then sifting the sugar and the ground rice together. It tasted delicious.

Shoggie looked in after lunch today, in his new RN uniform. He looked extremely smart, and told us all about his experiences in his ship. We had thought he was miles out to sea by now. He explained that he had indeed ventured out into the ocean waves with his sailors. He was forced to turn back after a buffeting gale arose. The chagrin on his face was too evident for us not to laugh.

Series of wet days. Went over to Ryde by train, and then had to send over to Sandown for waterproofs. By the time they arrived with Steakie—she brought Mr Barnes's for me—the rain had stopped. Ryde, after the torrential downpour, proved a most tiring place to walk about. Left half our shopping undone and retreated back to Sandown. Nannie very disappointed I had not got the black ribbons she wants to brighten up her brown bonnet.

The Bud had tea with us today and later accompanied us on a walk round Yaverland and Brading. He was passionately keen to see the Roman villa which was unearthed nine years ago when men were digging a

Our first attempt at making Scotch shortcake
~~Sat~~ Friday. 4th Oct.
1/4 lb. butter
1/4 lb. flour
1/4 lb. ground rice
10 spoons sifted sugar
pinch of salt

The Firm's last Sunday evening together. Oct. 20th
Between tea & church time

heepfold. Delightful mosaics over the floor — Orpheus harming the animals with his nusic, Perseus freeing ndromeda, Ceres handing the ruits of the earth to Triptolemus, nd many more. The Bud in aptures. Declared he wished he had been the one to find the villa. He would have lived in it and held wild Bacchanalia. Ushered him away before he became too affected by the villa's atmosphere. A group of bespectacled and bearded Germans who pored over each floor, referring to guide books every other minute, seemed deeply shocked by his flippancy.

Preparing to make my annual visit to York. Plan to stop off at Datchet to see Tykie and Charlie. Spent an amusing Sunday evening before departure with Lilian, Steakie and Noggie. Noggie is going away too, to London, and Lilian and Steakie to cousins in Sussex. We all tried on Lilian's new hat. Noggie looked by far the best in it. The Firm then went, in a very agreeable mood, to church, where the longest sermon ever preached served to dispel our good humour.

Lilian, Steakie, Noggie and I all left Sandown at 10.45 am. We had a very pleasant journey together as far as Woking. We had one of the guitars out, and sang duets and choruses. Arrived at Datchet in good time. Nobody there to meet me, as I was early. Left my traps, and walked to the Avenue. Met Charlie just setting off to collect me, and he went and fetched my trunk. Delighted to see Tykie. She looks very well and happy. We had a long chat after dinner. I told her all about my troubles with the Great G. She was deeply sympathetic, and confessed she had got married as much to leave her home as for any other reason.

Went up to London to a Jewish wedding. Beatrice Marks married Sydney Grosse in St Petersburgh Place. Very solemn affair. The bride looked wonderfully happy, if four inches taller than her groom. Very interested to see inside a synagogue. Afterwards, did a little shopping. Then went to the Savoy Hotel, where we were to stay overnight. Went to the Haymarket to see *One Man's Shadow*. By a coincidence, Major Brown was there. He came and sat beside us and treated us to tea in the interval. Afterwards, Charlie met us and we all had lemon squashes before going to roost. Very long and enjoyable day. My grey pelisse met with great admiration.

Did some shopping in Bond Street — evening gloves — and at the Army and Navy Stores — petticoats and camisoles. Lunched at the Alexandra Club, where Tykie is a much loved member. Lamb and broad beans. Returned happily to Datchet by the 4.45 pm train.

November 1889

Started for York at 1.15 pm today. Mrs Durlacher was at Datchet station, so travelled to Waterloo with her. Dudley met me at King's X. Read *Vanity Fair* on the train and consumed egg and cress sandwiches Tykie had supplied. Gave the chocolate to a small child who started to besiege her improvident mother with complaints of hunger when she saw me picnicking. Stopped her whining for a few miles. Arrived in York about 8 pm.

Went to the Market today. Overjoyed to see familiar faces. All the ladies of York busy about their shopping. Met Mrs Sydenham Walker, buying

Bobbing for Apples *At Lawrence House* *Saturday 2nd Nov.*

a mound of redcurrants for her famous jam. Promised me a jar for Nannie. Dancing class at Lawrence House, which I attended for fun. Bobbed for apples afterwards. My boa got soaked.

Painted in the morning at Mrs Walker's. She has taken up art as a hobby, also. In the afternoon, went to The Retreat, the mental asylum, to practise for the concert. In the evening, attended Mr Wallace's lecture on 'The Colours of Animals'.

Practised again at The Retreat for the concert in the evening. My voice not in its best shape. Dr Baker, the principal at The Retreat, told me affectionately that I sounded like a corncrake. My sagging confidence drooped a little more. Terrified I will dry up completely after the opening chord. Such a waste for all the people who have bought tickets. Drank a quart of hot lemon with honey to try and restore the *vox humana*. Worried what to wear. My black satin is not very gay. Foolishly, did not think to bring my Milkmaid outfit, which might have distracted the eye.

The Cares of a family on a muddy day *Friday Nov. 15*

The Retreat concert passed without a hitch. There was not a murmur from the audience when I sang 'Tell me, pretty maid', and my voice rang out clarion clear. A vast sum of money was made, so all the inmates will be able to enjoy therapeutic games of tennis, once the court is built.

Went to St Martin-cum-Gregory, in Micklegate, in the morning. Thought of all the mayors of York who are buried there. Perhaps it was the length of the sermons that led them to an early grave through boredom and cold. In the afternoon, we sat in the Minster nave during the service. Admired, as ever, the medieval glass depicting a king seated on the branches of a tree against a celestial blue background. Went to St Olave's, York's oldest church.

Lily North and I stayed in all day, neither the weather nor my cold propitious for outings. Failed to attend a concert in aid of the organ fund of St Martin-cum-Gregory.

Spent the day in bed.

Stayed in. Painted Christmas cards with Lily all afternoon. Stuck sweet little robins all over my card for Mrs Walker. Little Mathilda gave us a dreadful fright by suddenly appearing at the top of the stairs and announcing she was going to fly down, like the fairy in the pantomime.

The "pear of harmony" in the Market Place

Saturday. Nov. 9th

Tuesday. 26th Nov.
It is necessary to stir the Xmas pudding seven times without speaking, & to wish hard all the time — but how is it possible when Ginger insists on asking questions all the time?

Called to see Miss Kirby at the old school. Felt quite like a girl again in her presence, though my schooldays are long since over.

Tuesday Nov. 12th.
"Come! for my arms are empty!"
(as sung by special request)

Had tea with Mrs Walker and went with her to a Chrysanthemum Exhibition. The scent of the thousands of specimens made me quite faint. My first day out since my cold. Mrs Walker made me lie down outside the hall. Passers-by were amazed.

Had tea with Miss Kirby again. A delightful treat now, when it used to be a penance. Heard of several of the old girls. They almost all seem to be married now. Lily North and I are two of the few keeping the spinster standard flying. Lecture on 'Animal Locomotion' in the evening.

Made the Christmas pudding today—putting to use the largest pudding bowl the house possessed. We stirred and tasted and stirred all morning. Candied orange peel and candied figs were added this year as a special luxury. In among the mixture we buried tiny charms—a lucky boot and a little iron and a silver sixpence. We were hot and bothered when we had finished, but the pudding is made, and the Christmas festivities next month can proceeed with their accustomed regularity.

December 1889

Took my guitar out to tea at Mrs Paterson's. Played patience. Dined at Burton Terrace, and afterwards went to the theatre to see Kate Vaughan in *The Country Girl*. Enjoyed it immensely.

Called on Ada Gosling, now Drake. She has married very well, really, though there were hopes at one time that one of the chocolate barons, Messrs Rowntree or Terry, might snap her up. She has a sweet baby, called Violet. Seemed to occupy a great deal of her time. She did explain that I had caught her at a bad moment, as her nurse had just given notice and was going off to work for a titled pair in the country. Ada seemed very cross about it. She always was a little tetchy at school—perhaps this put off Mr Rowntree. Accepted a cup of tea—very pretty Royal Worcester china, but sadly chipped—and made my exit with speed. Will be thankful to return to the Island on one count. Very few of my friends there have attained the married state.

Went to St Martin-cum-Gregory. Walked down to the Blue Bridge after lunch. The Ouse is still my favourite river, if the Thames is grander in design. Went to the Minster in the afternoon, where I am almost sure I saw Douglas Meeres. What he may be doing in York, I do not know. A horrid boy pulled my boa off.

Mrs White took us to see the old Merchants' Hall. She told us that, in the last century, it had been used as a place of entertainment where gentlemen danced on ropes, tumbled and juggled. One man pushed a wheelbarrow with a child in it along a rope pulled taut, she told us, but we were not to be convinced. Told her of Shoggie's tricks. He can juggle three apples in the air at once. Afterwards, we went to Rowntrees' Japanese Room, the oldest room in York. Gave me several ideas for refurbishing my bedroom in Sandown.

Had tea with Miss Kirby, and, for old times' sake, went to St Peter's School Theatricals. Much enjoyed them. Brother Herbert was mentioned in the Epilogue. Wrote home to tell the Great G all about it.

Ada skated all morning, but I did not dare to venture on the ice. Went with Lily to buy Xmas cards in the afternoon. Then, helped Lily get the coffee ready for the Hungate women. Such a practical plan. All the poor Irish women come and have a cup dispensed to them. They find it a very cheering little luxury. Dance at The Retreat in the evening. Dr Baker danced with me several times. Very surprised, as we twirled round the room in a polka, to see Reggie Fox. Sat out the Swedish Dance with him, and talked over Sandown. Danced with Lily and Charlie Cooper, besides.

Started for Sandown at 10 am. Always sorry to leave York, and all the old friends. Glad to go back to my humdrum routine, none the less. Pleasant journey. The Firm came to meet me at the station, which was very cheering. No calamities have occurred while I have been away. Very tired, so Nannie brushed my hair for me in front of the fire tonight. Spent Christmas Eve opening parcels at Fernside. Both Lilian and Steakie brought theirs over to open with me. Very exciting results. Lily North gave me a conjuring set, with which you can all but magic rabbits out of hats. Mrs Walker gave three cakes of scented soap. Steakie had from her grandmother a garnet brooch, which she instantly pinned to her hat. Lilian had a leather-bound set of Shakespeare from an uncle

:hristmas Day. Early service with .ilian, and morning service at :hristchurch. Nannie came, ɔoking very smart in the muffler knitted her in York. :hurch Parade afterwards. We did ıot stay long, as Nannie tires easily. ;lad to see Reggie Fox back from 'ork, but Major Brown took the :hristmas cheer a little far. le insisted on kissing us all twice. ea at Collingbourne. Ruby had aved a cracker for me to pull vith her and we roasted hestnuts in the fire. Went to 1anor House to the Meeres boys' party at 8 pm. My first acquaintance with 'punch'. Heaven knows what went into it. Got home about quarter to twelve. Never had such a happy Christmas in my life.

Very cold grey day. Mollie and Maggie Boucher, Lilian, Steakie, Barbara Raxworthy, Douglas and Charlie Meeres all came to tea at Fernside. Not my idea. Nannie insisted I should ask them. Baked some biscuits which curled up and a cake which sagged in the middle. All were too polite to mention it. The Great G came in at five o'clock and sat down scowling at us. All soon left. Not a wild success.

Lilian and I and Uncle Ward walked out to look at the remains of the Norwegian barge, which was wrecked in the summer. It is a sad sight, beached on the sands. We spent the evening at the Jacobs'. Very amusing. We played all kinds of games under Colonel Jacob's aegis. Brewed punch on our return to Collingbourne. Bed at 1.30 am.

Spent a delightful New Year's Eve at the Bouchers. Drank each others' healths in champagne and reeled home to hear the grandfather clock chime twice. Thankfully, the Great G and Nannie did not wake as I stumbled my way to bed.

to Miss Barry singing
during the 3rd Lancers

Forming Attachments

1890 to 1891

January 1890

New Year's Day rather slow. Played the banjo, while the Great G snored and Nannie read. The cats were my only audience. Lilian and Noggie and I went for a cold wet stamp along the sea-wall. Noggie told us of his

Theatrical Night. Friday 3rd Jan.
Behind the curtain. "Mabel Charteris" (M.J.) dancing a bogus minuet with Parkinson (Major

dreams of going into the Army and becoming a General. We listened intently, but could not feel he was a military man. Not like Colonel Berkeley, for example.

Milder weather. Called on the Jacobs and also on the Hatchets. Georgie Jacob was busy with a young kitten which she had just saved from a damp death in the garden well. Sweet little mite. Had great difficulty detaching its claws from my boa. Georgie enticed it away with a dish of smoked haddock left over from luncheon in the end.

The Firm played tiddleywinks to brighten up a dull Thursday, Noggie cheated dreadfully, and nudged his counters round so that Lilian won. Pretended not to notice. Mixed a great many cordials together to make a loving cup, which we drank as we played.

)ress rehearsal at the Town Hall
t 2.30 pm of *Ici On Parle*
rancais. Then acted to a very
rowded house. Mabel was
pplauded con brio, as Lady
Charteris. I danced a bogus
ninuet with Parkinson, the butler,

"Flitterkins."

akie succumbs
to an irresistible
argument.

ehind the curtain. Very nearly
ipped over a rope which would
ave brought all the scenery
umbling about our ears.

igh jinks at Collingbourne.
ank and Steakie got into an
gument about how the Latin
g, *Veni, vidi, vici,* should be
ronounced. Frank got out the
oda water syphon to prove his
oint, and Steakie succumbed to
is irresistible argument.
e crowed like a turkey cock.
eizing the opportunity to complete
s dominance over his sisters, he
tacked Lilian at her guitar with
e poker. Thankfully, there were
calamities. As it was so wet a
y, we whiled away some more
ours playing flitterkins.
ttle Ruby Barnes was much
nused by our dexterity.

Went for another cold, wet stamp on the seafront. Lilian and I seriously discussed our old plan to go to Germany on a Grand Tour. Finances argue against it, we had to admit reluctantly. Lilian has £3 6s, I have two guineas.

Fought my way through the rain to Collingbourne, where Daisy Jones and Barbara Raxworthy did some tableaux. Barbara was particularly good as 'The Lady of Shalott'. We all applauded vigorously when she lay down on the drawing-room sofa and Daisy pushed her down river, as it were, on this barge. Most unfortunately, Mrs Barnes happened to come in while we were all in fits, and objected strenuously to the damage the play was causing to her carpet.

Walked with Barbara along the sea-wall in the morning. She had much to tell about the Thompson row which still continues. Echoes of it resound all around Sandown. Mrs Hatchet is said to

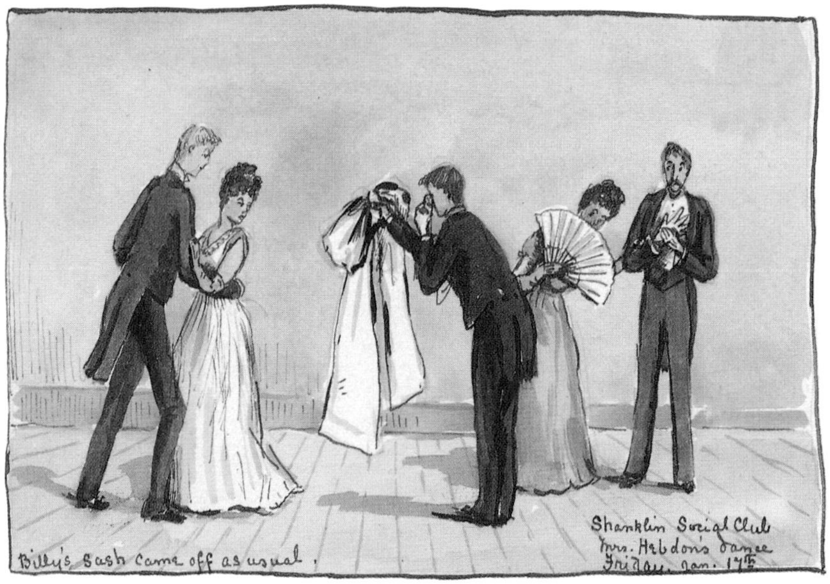
Billy's sash came off as usual.
Shanklin Social Club
Mrs. Hebdon's dance
Friday. Jan. 17th

have consulted Granny Price in her stone hut on the hill. Lilian, Steakie and I eagerly await further developments.

The Great G has gone to bed with the gout. Very upsetting for all of us, especially as his temper does not improve with illness. Nannie and I took turns to read *The Times* to him.

Went over to Ryde with Lilian and Steakie and Noggie. Bought several bobbins and needles. Planning to embroider some covers for the cushions in the Great G's study. Thought noughts and crosses, worked in white on a black ground, might give suitable nuances of his past career at St Peter's.

Ernest Frere came over to ask us to Mrs Hebdon's dance at the Shanklin Social Club. She has not given one before, being a retiring sort of creature. It is for her niece from London. Appropriately pleased, and sent messages of thanks. Deliberated what to wear. Decided in the end on the White Moth dress I wore last year to the Fancy Dress. The dance did not pass without the customary accident—Lilian's sash came off while she was dancing with Noggie. Called on Mrs Hebdon after the dance, or meant to , but our courage failed us at the last, and we sent in Noggie with our cards.

Our courage having failed us at the last
we ignominiously sent Noggie in with our cards

February 1890

Basking in the sun on the Esplanade in the morning.

Lilian and I went to Christchurch this morning, Lilian wearing a very neat new hat. Mrs Hatchet turned round to see what the fuss was about—Lilian having dropped her prayer book—and looked perfectly black with rage. At our frivolity, I suppose.

Took Nannie in the donkey-cart down to the esplanade, where we basked in the sunshine.

Lilian and Noggie sat on the rails overlooking the sea. Our thoughts turned to the land across the main, and to our plans to go to Germany. Longing to walk in the Black Forest, but Nannie became quite agitated when she heard us discussing our plan. She cannot bear any mention of 'abroad'.

Lilian drove with Mrs Barnes over to Ryde this afternoon, so I was left to my own devices. Wrote two letters, and painted two firegrates with Aspinall's Superior Terracotta Enamel Paint.

Too wet today to do anything, so we both, Lilian and I, kept ourselves very busy, painting a bookshelf. Terrible trouble, painting round our feet. Though we both wore huge aprons, we still contrived to deposit a large part of the enamel over ourselves.

At Collingbourne, Mr Barnes promised me a pair of gloves if I would kiss him. Lilian kissed him pretending to be me. He was not to be taken in by this base fraud. Resolved he should be my Valentine for this year.

Had a really hard guitar practice together in the afternoon. Poor Billy had a bad blister on her finger, as a result, and was not able to play at all later. I had to sustain the credit of The Firm by performing alone at Mrs Hardy's.

A Wet Afternoon. Billy & I find ourselves very busy.

Trying to get a pair of gloves out of Mr Barnes by a base fraud. Billy kissed him, & pretended I had, but he was not to be taken in.
2nd February

Mrs Hardy had her dance tonight. There were hardly any men there, so Mrs Hardy said we were to dance together. Only too eager. It was the greatest of fun.

Met Mollie, who told us that poor Noggie had fallen victim to the Russian influenza. Very worrying. Debated whether to visit him, and decided best not. Persuaded Lilian, who was very eager, that a few days might well elapse before we went to see him, and it would still not be the end of the world.

Went round the Common with Lilian, warmly wrapped up in rugs. Very blowy weather. We discussed whether to have raspberry or blackcurrant jam for tea — a very important matter which took us right round the Common and back to Fernside.

Went to see Noggie, who is convalescent. Persuaded by his example to down large glasses of maraschino, on the understanding 'Prevention is better than cure'.

"Only a Face at the Window"
Thursday Feb. 6th

Thursday. Feb 6th
After Mrs. Hardy's 'musical Evening'

In the afternoon, wandered about the house under the impression that I was busy packing. Very excited at the prospect of seeing Beatrice and Charles and Toddie again.

Valentine's Day. Got the prettiest little brooch — bog oak with pearls — from Lilian. Sweet little Nannie gave me a sovereign. It will go towards the fund for Germany, though I did not tell her that. Mr Barnes very pleased with the card I made him.

There were hardly any men so Mrs. Hardy said we were all to dance together
Mrs. Hardy's dance
Saturday. Feb. 8th
I bravely hauled the "Indian Brave" round in the mazy dance

The Butler

Billy's Valentine.

Lilian came with me over to Portsmouth and then I proceeded alone to Datchet. There were some very unruly children in the carriage—quite without the care of any nurse, it seemed—who threw paper bags of toffees out of the window. I watched, helpless to intervene. Dear Tykie met me at Datchet. She had stuck a flower in her hat which made greetings rather difficult. We managed to stow all my baggage in the donkey-cart, and rushed off to the Avenue. Heard all the plans for moving to the new house. Sorry to see them go, really, from the Avenue. Such pleasant memories of high jinks over the years.

Celebrated my arrival with a hot punch of wine and herbs. Mr Bingham, a nice bachelor of the parish, came to dinner. Very charming, but would talk of nothing but his pigs. This made dinner a wearing business. Went to a concert in aid of the Fire Brigade after dinner and returned to drink more punch. Charlie and Mr Bingham did so much tasting, we thought it best to carry it off upstairs.

Monday 17th Feb.
Having just stuck a new flower in her hat — with one pin only — There was a little stiffness observable in Tykie's greeting.

a passing glimpse of my valentine

Wed. 12th Feb.
making the best of the

Monday. 17th Feb.
Removing The punch-bowl

"The Influenza Scare"
"Prevention is better than cure" but our remedy is not the one generally recommended by The Faculty.
(maraschino)
Thursday 13th Feb.

Uncle Bennie joined us today, fresh from London. He is so tall, it is a wonder that his tailor can find cloth long enough to fit him. A very welcome adjunct to the party. He took us all into Windsor and bought Tykie and me ices. We were delighted. When we came home, he took up the banjo and fairly let rip. We did have a merry time.

Took the train over to Thorpe. Ted met us and made us very welcome. We had wild games of cards and whist. Beatrice got in a temper, because her pile of jettons was smaller than anyone else's, and ended by overturning the table in her frustration.

Friday 21st Feb
The relative sizes of "Uncle Bennie" & myself

Thursday Afternoon Feb. 20th
Rest under difficulties at Thorpe.

This is how Tykie started for her ride on Saturday Morning. Feb. 22nd
This "large creature" is meant to represent a pony.

Windsor. Saturday 22nd Feb.
marching with the soldiers.

Our Banjo Concert at Thorpe. Thursday Evening Feb. 20th

Tykie and I listened all evening to musical selections on the banjo. I assisted with original renderings of the pianoforte accompaniments. It was a very jolly evening. Eastley End such an extremely distinguished house.

Came back to the Avenue, Datchet. Charlie and Tykie went for a ride after breakfast. I walked into Windsor and back. The band was playing. I marched along with the soldiers, so as to hear as much as possible. So inspiring, to hear our brave soldiers trumpeting their devotion to the Sovereign. Would have liked to go riding with Charlie and Tykie, but they did not propose a mount. Truth to tell, I don't know how to ride, but I would have welcomed the offer.

Spent the afternoon choosing patterns for the Red House, and began to dismantle the drawing-room. Sad to think of Charlie and Tykie leaving the Avenue. Such happy times there.

Felt a little put out that Tykie did not seem to value my help in choosing patterns. I had selected to be a pony and clip-clopping all over the house. So fortunate she married Charlie, and finally realised her dream of owning two or three horses.

Got terribly lost, coming back to Portsmouth. Fortunately, met Mr Powell all of a sudden, who directed me to the boat. Asked me to have a cup of tea with him at Keppel's Head, but declined. Had an inkling it would have been thought rather fast. Should really like to know if it would have been proper.

"The wreck of a once happy home

Saturday. 22nd Feb.

a dusky pink wallpaper with embossed swans which I thought would give a charming effect in the new drawing-room. Tykie said she would feel as if she were engulfed by a pond. She selected, instead, a yellow stripe. Walked into Windsor to buy a model of the castle for young Ruby Barnes.

Charlie went off to a whist party after dinner, so Tykie and I sat and talked over old times in the library. Remembered when we were girls, and Tykie used to infuriate her family by pretending

Saturday Feb. 22nd
Choosing pattern for "The Red House" – our usual occupation.

March 1890

Feel rather miserable today. Lilian has gone off to stay with Lucy Gates again, and I am left to my own devices. Tried painting a bracket, to while away the hours, but it did not answer. Feel quite widowed without her. Colder than ever, and snow on the ground.

My last lonely walk. Monday 10th March
(I took a stamp on the sea-wall after meeting the 3.30 train, & before meeting the 4.30 train)

Went down to the station to meet six trains before my dearest Lilian condescended to arrive. Happiest of arrivals. Felt so glad to see her, my whole day transformed.

Monday 3rd March.
Rushing down to the 1.30 train with a small parcel.

Rushed into Ryde to do some shopping. Took in the grey frock for Mrs Boucher. Met Gladdis in the Ryde waiting-room. He had the good news that Captain Gordon means to open the Club now for a time, while the weather is dry. Wonderful idea. Much look forward to it, and to improving my tennis.

Took Nannie for a short walk in the afternoon, and then had tea at Collingbourne. Mrs Barnes and Nannie had a passionate talk about the knitting patterns they use. Nannie trounced Mrs Barnes by showing her an armhole which was quite clearly superior in style. Mrs Barnes responded by throwing her pattern in the fire and demanding Nannie's.

We spent the day today making toffee with vinegar. It took hours for it to stiffen. We whiled away the time practising songs for the Town Hall concert.

Nannie liked our toffee so much, she asked us to make some more. We found making a larger quantity entailed much more work. We were quite exhausted by the end, as we took turns at stirring it. Annie is ill in bed with influenza, besides, so a large part of the cooking and washing up has devolved on yours truly.

Annie is still ill and the Great G suffering from the gout. Things in general rather a woeful ash-heap.

Lilian and I went to Yaverland and back. Had a mysterious bill from Briggs & Co. for umbrellas £20 worth. Seemed almost too comical to be annoying.

Took a solemn constitutional along the esplanade. Wondered if we would still be doing the same, five years hence. When we were telling our fortunes the day before yesterday, it seemed that a dark, handsome stranger would soon cross my path. A black cat darted out in front of us, which might well be what was augured.

Lilian and I decided the times were so bad, we should cheer ourselves up with that old and

Friday March 14th
Taking turns to stir the toffee

tested remedy—a picnic. Accordingly, we took some hard-boiled eggs and made our way, pursued by a gusty wind, to Whitecliff Bay. Here we rested and took our ease, till a large cow poked its muzzle round a furze bush and startled us on our way. Not before I had made a little sketch of the Bay, however, with which I was mightily pleased.

April 1890

Lovely fine day. The sea rough, however. Heard reports that there had been an accident at sea. Dreadfully perturbed to think our brave seamen might have perished but, as luck would have it, it turned out to be a boatful of French chefs from Boulogne. They were out pleasure jaunting, when their boat capsized. They were able to send up a rocket, and so were rescued—all but their chefs' hats—by our Lifeboat men. O dangers of the English main.

Noggie's 21st birthday today. I made him a pipe cleaner out of two strands of wire which I plaited together. Lilian gave him a pair of slippers on which she had embroidered two little pigs. He paid us the delicate compliment of saying that we, between us, had ensured his early retirement from the world. He had only to put his feet on the fender and he would be quite the grandpapa. To celebrate the event, we took the train to Alverstone, and then walked to Knighton Woods. They were very beautiful, all the blossom just now springing into bloom. Georgie Jacob, always the *enfant terrible*—she refuses to put up her hair, though she is past nineteen—got an ashen club and began to belabour the blossom above our heads till we were all covered with it. We picked several basketfuls of primroses, some for the Easter decorations and some for our homes. The high point of the outing, though, was the picnic. Mollie Boucher had made some

Thursday. 3rd April
(Primrosing excursion to Knighton)
Lunch time! – drinking Noggie's health,
it being his 21st birthday.

delicious ham patties.
Noggie, Lilian and I walked home along the railway-line, singing songs all the way.

Colonel Jacob met us this morning and urged us to come and look at his photo in

This is not a free fight — it is only "Animal Grab." Sat. 5th April

Debenham's. We each insisted on having one. Went over to Collingbourne for tea, and had an uproarious game of Animal Grab.

Thirteen of us, all told, went over the Dockyard and had tea with Uncle Ward on HMS *Vernon*. Mrs Barnes, Lilian, me, Frank, Miss Nicholson — whom I found entrancing — Mr Boucher, Mollie and Fred and Miss Allen, Alice Neal, Ethel Hargrove, Hartie Stainthorpe and Mr Duke. We all had a rattling good time.

The Primrose League Entertainment this evening. Lilian and I wore *gitana* dresses which we copied from the ballet, *Giselle*. Major Brown, who was producing the show, said he thought we looked like two Carmens, which we considered a rather fast remark. Drank a thimbleful of Dutch courage before we went on. Rapturous applause.

Had tea at the Jacobs'. Georgie sang some sea shanties and Colonel Jacob presented me with some lettuces before I came away. Met Mrs Boucher in the town, who gave me to understand that Noggie has got the influenza again. Lilian most concerned, and vowed she would make him a hot posset. Mrs Barnes looked quite askance at her.

Indecision
Saturday April 12th
5 minutes before the train goes!

Partaking of Dutch Courage
Thursday. April 10th

En Route for Bambridge. Rest on the way – Sunday Afternoon. April 13th

May 1890

Beautiful day. We climbed up to the top of the railway bridge in the afternoon and had a splendid view of the carriages returning from Ashey Races. Whenever anyone passed whom we knew, we lay low.

Watching the carriages pass after the races
Thurs. May 1st

We "lay low" on the bank of the sea-wall

The Sandown Fund.
Attack by the Enemy.
Tuesday 6th May.

The Firm and Noggie and Mollie Boucher chose this morning to take our walk along the sea-front at a leisurely pace. Tired after the tennis on Saturday. Unfortunately, as we sat down to rest on a bench, the Enemy, in the shape of Mrs Hatchet, appeared. She roundly told us off for lounging when we could have been doing good works or taking exercise. Noggie invited her to sit down with us, but this only inflamed her further and she strode off in a huff.

Did the Coal and Clothing Club this morning. Took hours. Mrs Jenkins came, bearing all the clothes we had issued her with. Seems none of them fitted her bairns. Gave her another load, of jersey dresses. Feel she is really trying to be difficult. Bea Frere sent over from Shanklin to ask us to tea at the Social Club. Very enjoyable. Discussed the interesting question of how Noggie would fare in the Army. Lilian very silent for once.

Went for a long walk with a Mr Cumming, whom we met at the Shanklin Social Club, and who has come to the Island for a rest cure. Walked to Godshill Park, in the course of which we met a

Not exactly monotonous but near it!

Invitations came for the dance on HMS *Vernon*. We must have made a good impression. Sadly, Mrs Barnes is ill, so we cannot go. No other chaperone can be found. Cheered ourselves with a rousing game of Animal Grab.

Started a bad throat, so did not go out again after morning church. A pity, as Mrs Meataxe descended on us, and offered her services as chaperone for the *Vernon* dance. Refused, not being willing to submit to her authority, but oh, I do wish we could go.

newly tarred fence. Mr Cumming of no use whatsoever! We managed to evade the tea and tramped further to Appuldurcombe. There we saw Mrs Pope. Sadly, Harold was out. Had tea, but, though we lingered, he did not return. At least, he did not come in to join us. As Mrs

Pope was pouring my second cup of tea, I distinctly heard movements in the hall and mutterings. So perhaps he did come in but felt too tired to join us. Harold, I know, has very delicate feelings, and would hesitate to come in if he were not feeling quite up to the mark.

Wednesday. 14th May.
On our way to Godshill Park we met a newly-tarred fence.

June 1890

Thursday. 12th June

Friday 13th June
We took it in turns to hold up a gargantuan umbrella while the other admired the effect.

Come to Datchet to stay with Charlie and Tykie for the Races. Adore Tykie's new house. It is quite lovely, red Elizabethan brick and mullioned windows. Reminds me somewhat of Hampton Court. Tykie distinctly flattered when I mentioned this. A dinner party tonight, with Lady Langrishe the chief guest. Very droll. We played billiards after dinner. Sir James Langrishe very *épris* in Tykie's direction.

Charlie had to go to London on business, so Tykie took me out for a ride in the donkey-cart. It would have been very pleasant, only the reins broke, and we were very nearly deposited on the verge.

Helped her 'sort out' the tea room this afternoon. She has made gargantuan umbrellas to give it a Japanese effect, and we had the greatest of fun trying to decide just where they should go. One almost ended by landing on my head, such was my enthusiasm to help and Tykie's tendency to hesitate before approving a site.

The country around Datchet most fetching. White painted gates sit within laburnum hedges, and fields of potatoes and wheat make agreeable land through which to walk. Charlie and Tykie ride out every morning. Tykie has a dashing charger named Woolly, which has a worrying habit of rearing and prancing when she mounts. Still no suggestion that I join them, so I take my pleasures on foot. Did mention to Tykie that

Tykie took me for a drive in the donkey-cart, & the reins broke.

I would be glad to learn to ride—Harold Pope has a large stable at Appuldurcombe—but no very forthcoming answer.

Drove over to Thorpe in the afternoon. Beatrice very happy to see us and Eastly End looking grey and stately in the summer heat. Dined and stayed the night, and painted the verandah chairs in the morning.

My trousseau from Mrs Gibbon has proved invaluable on this visit. Tykie and Charlie have the widest possible acquaintance and there has been a procession of eligible bachelors through the house. Made great play with my new feather fan, which amused Charlie. He swore I had captured Captain Curl's heart, but I rebuffed such nonsense.

The Duke has come to stay for Ascot Races. He arrived very late on Monday evening, and , as he is very superstitious, we engaged a sweep to take him his early morning tea. His language was plain. We all heard it, and Charlie was moved to jump out of his bath and enquire, in very forcible tones, what the dickens was going on.

After breakfast, we all set out for the Races and had a very jolly drive. Tykie wore mauve, Mrs Young an elegant black-and-white stripe, and I wore grey and white. We felt we were a credit to the menfolk, and they showed their partiality by treating us to a very good luncheon. I saw several friendly faces in the Royal Enclosure, and enjoyed myself enormously. The third race of the afternoon was my triumph, when Morion, the horse I had backed with Charlie, came in first. We had champagne in a tent to celebrate. Poor Charlie was not in the best of moods, as I had accidentally dented his top hat with my parasol handle in my enthusiasm at winning. In the tent, Tykie was jostled by a burly, moustachioed officer, and her champagne went all over Charlie's coat. As I pointed out, his racing glasses were not touched, and the damage to the coat was not irreparable. I fear Charlie was not entirely convinced by these arguments. He whipped poor Junius along without mercy on our return. Perhaps it was not anger but merely the excitement of the afternoon's racing which had left him with dreams of being a jockey. We had a most relaxing end to the day, Charlie resplendent in a new quilted satin smoking jacket, and Roulette the feature of the evening. I sat next to the Duke and staked exactly as he did. The consequence was

that I won twenty-four shillings. I am thinking of buying a new hat, with plumes, to celebrate.

Meant to have returned to Sandown but having such a jolly time, decided not to. Drove over to Thorpe. Beatrice still suffering from a dreadful headache, but Ted happy to see us. Played guessing games all evening. Such a jolly household, even if the tread of little feet has not yet made happy their home. Wang, the Chinese boy, makes as many blunders as though he were a child. He brought gravy to the dinner table on Tuesday and tried to spoon it over our apricot tart.

Feel I must return to Sandown. Fretting a little to think how the household will be getting on without me. Started from Egham, a pleasant ride, only a small child threw my ticket out of the window. Had to give my name and address each time the tickets were collected.

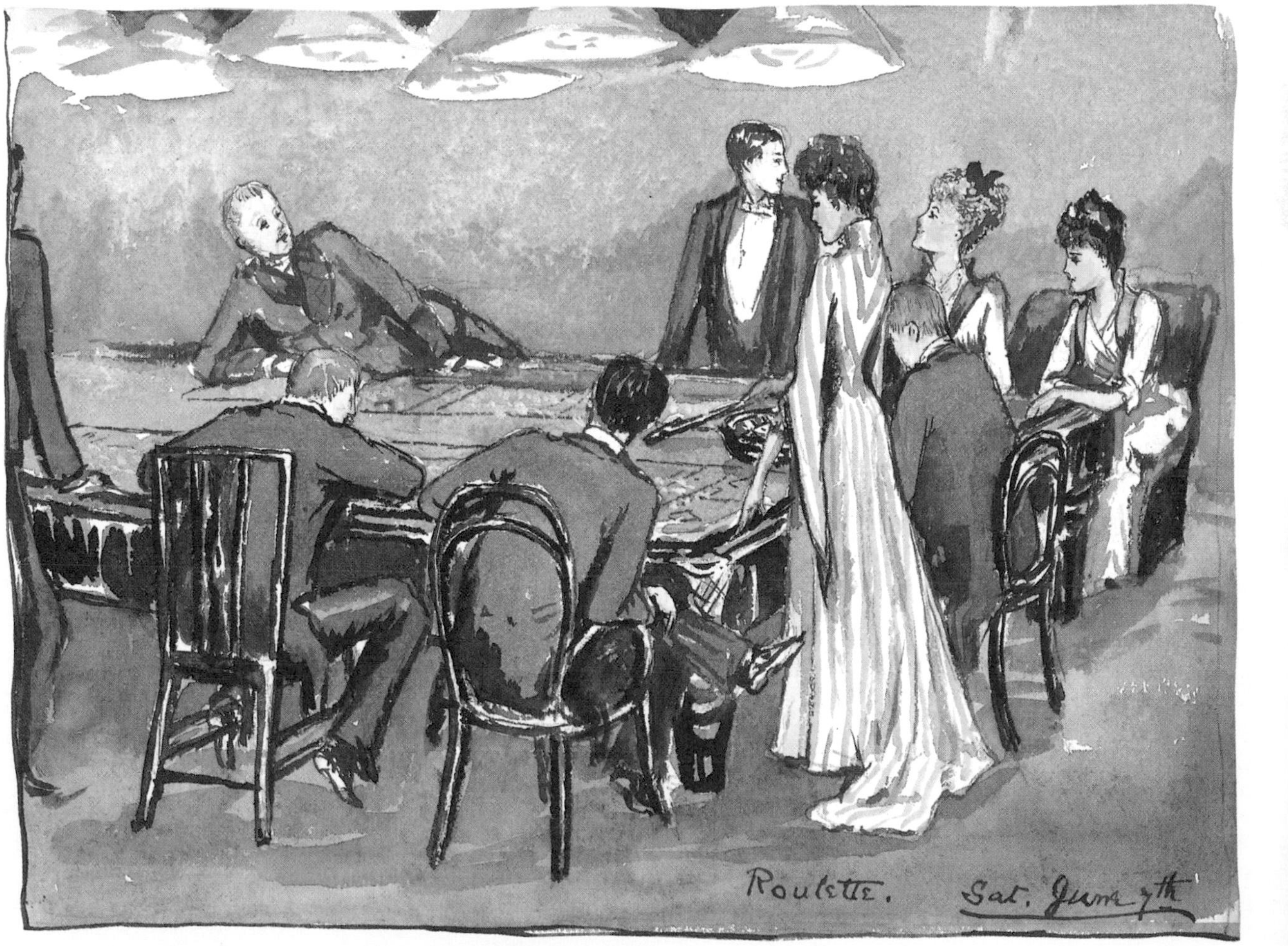

July 1890

Nice to be home. The parents both well. Nannie has crocheted a new skull-cap for the Great G. It fits him very well, and would make him look quite distinguished if Nannie's eyesight had not let her down. It is bright pink. Met Shoggie in the High Street, with a basket of strawberries. He persuaded me to sample some. Quite delicious. The treat only marred by a most disapproving glance from the Meataxe, passing by with her shopping.

Lilian and I are busy this week, improving our tennis. We are to play in a tournament on Saturday. Steakie has been commandeered by the Shanklin Tennis Club and made an honorary member, so that she can play for them against Ryde.

Read, as usual, to Emmie in the afternoon. We are still reading Renan's *Life of Jesus*. She is such a splendid invalid and never protests about the speed at which I read. As Renan is perhaps not the most interesting of writers, I tend to go rather fast. Went to the Club and had two sets of tennis with Noggie against Steakie and Mr Sigmond. Noggie improves all the time. Then we went to the Jacobs' for tea. Very pretty china, blue with gold trimmings. Georgie Jacob gesticulated so wildly, describing a house she had seen in Scotland, that she almost upset all our cups. Colonel Jacob was so kind as to give me a tobacco plant. We had strawberries for tea.

Went for a sail in the Wonga. Great fun, though Major Brown's idea of steering was not all one would have liked. We managed to bring the craft into the shore, but only just. Our petticoats and the hems of our dresses were soaked.

Went for another sail. O the swell of the ocean wave. Dared Major Brown to jump in and swim, but oddly, he refused to oblige.

Sunday 20th July
Cockchafers on the way home from Shanklin Church.

A fine Sunday at last. Lilian and I went on Church Parade in the morning, and saw many friends. Mrs Hatchet was also present. Horrid walk home on account of the cockchafers. They fluttered all about us.

Played three sets of tennis with Mr Peacock against Miss Peacock and Lilian, which became quite an exhausting adventure.
Mr Peacock is quite as proud as his namesake and refused to allow Lilian and Miss Peacock the benefit of the doubt in any line call.

Meant to have gone out in the Wonga, but it was too rough at sea. Played several sets of tennis, instead. Mr Peacock is distinctly good, despite his faults. Wore my new tennis costume for the first time.

Badminton tea-party at the Peacocks. Alice and Mary Neal were there, and were, as usual, disputing which of them should use the new racquet.
Georgie Jacob also appeared. Do wish she would put up her hair.

Not played badminton for some time. Worried my partners dreadfully by shying and turning my back on the shuttlecock whenever it came near.

Escorted the Great G and Nannie over to Portsmouth, to speed them well on their journey to Tunbridge wells. Hope they will have a really good rest.
The house seems very empty without them.

Played three sets of tennis with Captain Gordon and Lilian and young Gordon Maclaren.
Captain Gordon did a war dance every time he won a point. No sense of dignity, though he is the Secretary of the Club. Afterwards, we climbed on the Neals' railings to see the Carnival Procession. Little Ruby Barnes was there, dressed as a white rabbit. Went down to the High Street then, to watch the Procession go up the road.

Received two exquisite fans—one inlaid with mother-of-pearl, one of finest ebonite—from Madame Erazuriz, also an exquisite photo. Sad I cannot write to thank her, but there is no address given. A woman whose past and future are equally wrapped in mystery.

August 1890

Uniform
Wednesday 6th Aug

We all went down the Prom in uniform today, Mollie, Lilian, Steakie and I. Mollie was in such high spirits, she declared she felt like going swimming. We dissuaded her from this adventurous plan.

Colonel Atherley at the County Ground Sports
Monday. Aug. 4th

Went into Ryde with Lilian to do a little shopping. Bought some knitting wool, and some needles. Planning to make some little bootees for Edith's baby in York. Tired of playing whist every evening after dinner with the Great G and Nannie.

Tournament at the Club. Miss Collingwood gave the prize — two chatelaine scent-bottles. We all played our hardest for such a desirable offering, but were bested by Douglas Maclaren and Georgie Jacob, who carried off the prize. Douglas, not surprisingly, waived all rights to the prize, and Georgie carried off both bottles in triumph.

All the men have gone over to Cowes to see the fireworks. Sorely tempted to go with them, but caution prevailed. None of the other girls in the least keen. Heard from Harold Pope that there was to be a gigantic display of feathers to mark the popularity of the Prince of Wales. Wondered that he did not seem more keen to take me.

Played tennis with Miss Richardson, a rather dull match as my partner would complain that her new racquet was difficult to wield. After doubles with Miss Richardson, Lilian and Steakie, a

Carisbrooke Pic-nic. Wednesday. Aug. 20th
There were so many wasps about the table when we were getting the tea ready, that it was thought dangerous to trust me with the crockery, so I was told off to entertain the two children

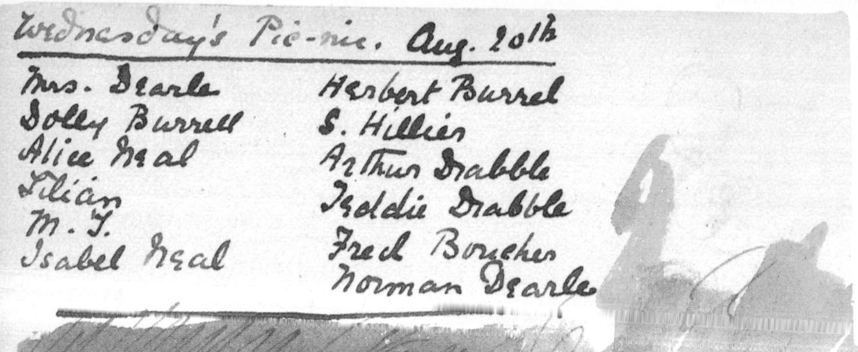

lower game of tennis with Lilian
ınd Noggie and Shoggie. All of us
ather tired of the Club. Caught at
ne suggestion of a picnic to
:arisbrooke castle, which Mrs
Hatchet is getting up. She means
ɔ take all the Sunday School
hildren. Thinking of making
ome gingerbread or some more
cotch shortbread as a treat
ɔr them.

ıvitations came for Mrs Pope's
ance at Appuldurcombe.
Iarold back from business in
ondon. Lilian, Steakie and I had
a conference and decided to wear white silk. Harold Pope danced with me twice and I distinctly saw Mrs Pope purse her lips the second time of asking. Felt this might be an omen. Danced till four in the morning.

We all set off for Carisbrooke castle in a wagonette, little Ruby Barnes and Edmund Neal—a most troublesome boy—sitting in the front, pretending to drive the vehicle themselves. When we got to the castle, there were so many wasps about the table that it was thought dangerous to trust me with the crockery. I was directed to entertain the children. Made daisy chains in the shelter of a fortified wall. Wonderful picnic, barring an accident when Arthur Drabble got up unexpectedly, and the bench deposited me abruptly on the ground.

Regatta today. I hate regattas. A fearful din going on all day on the Prom—hurdy-gurdies, concertinas, bagpipes, German brass bands and the town band. Went out for a short while, saw Georgie Jacob dancing along, with her petticoats flying, beside a hurdy-gurdy man. Colonel Jacob would have been shocked to see it.

Dull day. Went with Lilian and Fred (Noggie) to Shanklin church. Mrs Hatchet there in a monstrous hat, betrimmed and beribboned with vast curling plumes. Came out before the sermon.

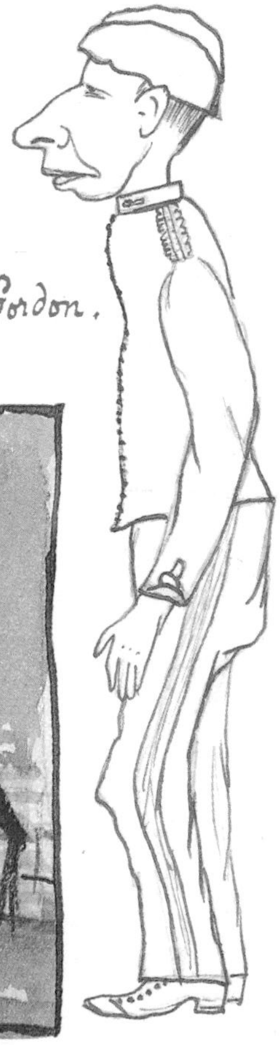

"Friend Robinson" drawn by Captain Gordon.

September 1890

Played a great deal of tennis this month. Have practised so much that I decided to enter the Ryde Open Tournament. No sooner had I put my name down than I was roundly defeated by the hopeless Daisy Fardell. Too late to withdraw my name.

Friday. Sept. 12th. Ryde Open Tournament.
I had to borrow George Fardell's hat to keep the sun out of my eyes.

Had a set at the Club today with Steakie against Lilian and Mabel. Then with Mabel against Lilian and Steakie. Started a set with Lilian against Mabel and Steakie. On our return home, Lilian suggested to me a daring plan. She wanted to go to the Fair in Sandringham Avenue. I am always ready for any prank with Lilian. A splendid adventure. Had a swing in a swingboat and then a shy at a cocoa-nut. Hurried home, though, when two coarse looking individuals began to follow us around the fairground

Played three sets with Major Brown against Lilian and Fred. They won, 6-2, 6-1, 4-6.
They make a rather demonic pair, as they seem to know each other's mind. Major Brown wasted point after point as we both called 'Yours' whenever a difficult ball winged its way over the net. Noggie's balletic leaps about the court a joy to see.

Thurs. Sept. 4th
Smith gave us each a piece of bridecake to dream on.
So we had to walk upstairs backwards way.

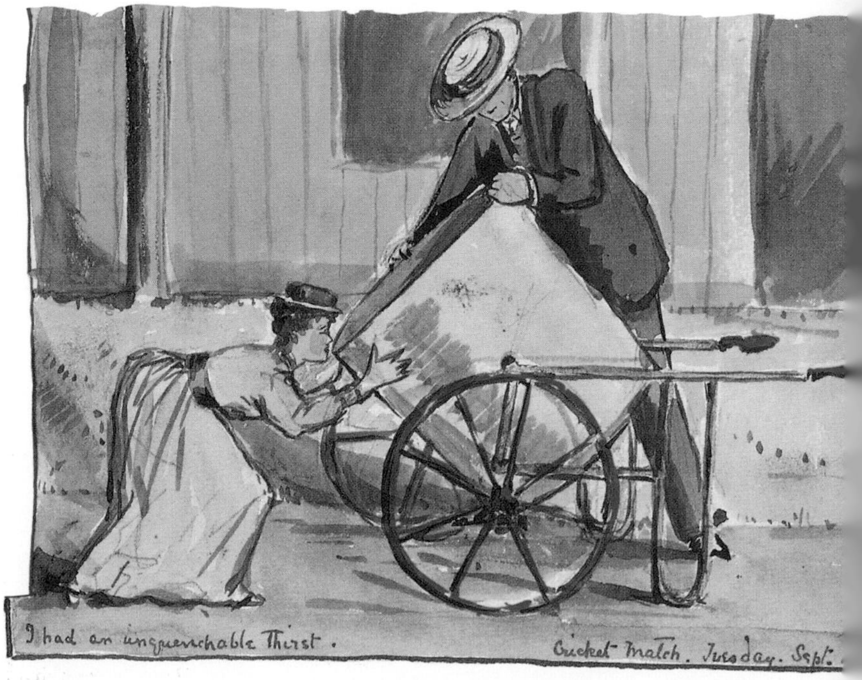
I had an unquenchable Thirst.
Cricket Match. Tuesday. Sept.

Cricket Match Tuesday. 16th Sept. Frank gave us a few instructions about how to bat.

Tues. Sept. 16th
I was surprised & hurt to be only allowed to bowl one "over" after displaying such astonishing style.

Did some dress-making in the morning and then relieved Lilian at the Coal and Clothing Club for half an hour. Went to the Smith's Reception in the afternoon. Alice Smith gave us each a piece of bride-cake to dream on, so we had to walk upstairs backwards.

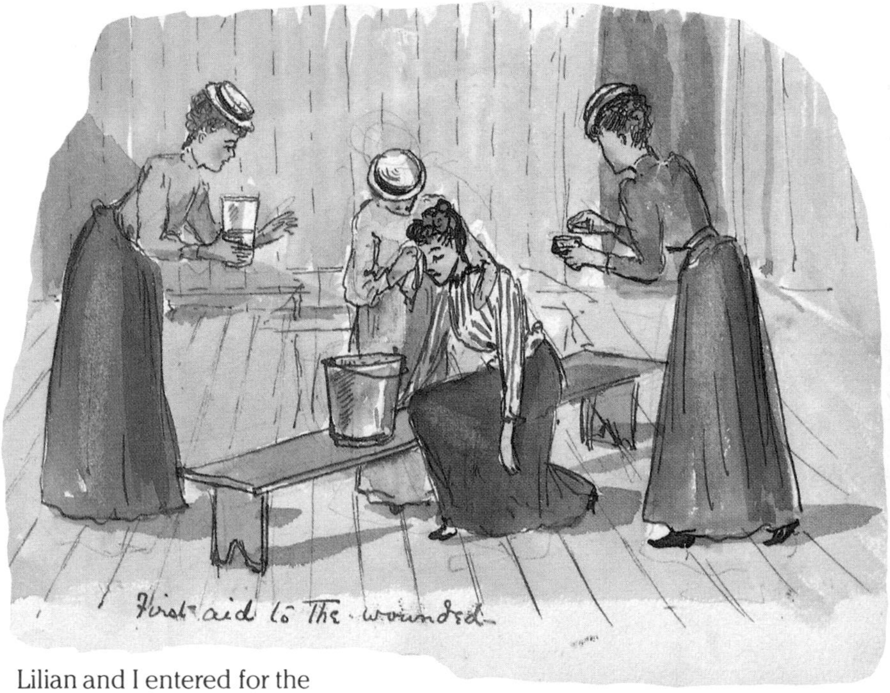

Lilian and I entered for the Ladies' Doubles at Ryde. Had to borrow George Fardell's hat to keep off the sun, it was so hot. Beaten in the second round.

Went to a big garden party at the Fardells'. Very superior. A band, ices, champagne cup and peaches. Did my duty by everything. About a hundred people.

I made my debut in a ladies' cricket match on the County Ground—Shanklin versus Southsea. Our team was Beatrice Frere, Lilian, Mabel and Steakie Barnes, Miss Way, Jessie and May Gordon, Miss Kelly, Dora Ernsthausen and M.T. We won. Although I went out with a duck in our first innings, I retrieved my reputation by making, in the second, thirteen runs and carrying my bat out. Agreeably surprised to find myself 'still alive and prowling'.

The Great G in a bate about something. Dreadfully stiff after yesterday's cricket. Lilian came over in the afternoon to assist me to read *Vanity Fair* to the Great G and Nannie. Horrid day, with a sea-fog which eventually turned to rain. Went to Shanklin church in the evening.

October 1890

Rather jolly scenes at the Tennis Club. Had the usual Last Day Frivol with five on each side. Lilian, however, much exercised, as she confessed to me afterwards, by a letter she has had from Noggie. She seemed disinclined to frivol, which rather put me off. Leapt about the court, none the less. Noggie wrote in his letter, it seems, of a pretty girl called Miss Fenwick who, he thought, had been at school with Lilian. Lilian said that if it was the only Miss Fenwick she remembered from Miss Peabody's, Noggie's eyesight must be playing him up. She had had a snub nose, goggle eyes, and an unnerving tendency to stammer. Feel it was rather tactless of Noggie to have mentioned this poor unfortunate in such glowing terms—especially when the situation between him and Lilian is still unresolved.

Went out under an armed guard of umbrellas to taste the sea air. Met Georgie Jacob, who was standing, arms akimbo, and hair flying in the rain—without any waterproof or umbrella—all by herself on the Prom. When I asked her what in the world she was doing, she started and replied she was called out of Peterscombe by elemental forces. She had been reciting 'Kubla Khan' to the waves. Begged her to consider her health and return home, but she remained immobile and obdurate.

Horrid day today. We mooned round and felt depressed till evening. The only light in the sky was when Georgie Jacob came over with a proposal that we go mushrooming at dawn. We hastily rejected her plan. Lilian confided to me her doubts about Fred's intentions while Steakie read, with her feet up on the sofa, some modern work entitled 'A Woman's Place is Not in the Home'. Wondered aloud where, in that case, it was, but Steakie only looked mysterious. Feel she is taking New Woman literature rather too seriously. Hope she does not cherish any dreams of making a convert out of me.

at the end of the season it is fatal to send Mabel or Steakie to field balls — as the black berries are ripe.

LAWN TENNIS TOURNAMENT AT RYDE.

We give the results of the three days' lawn tennis tournament at the Terrace Gardens below. The play was watched by large numbers of spectators. The Gardens were looking at their best, and lovely weather made the meeting a most successful one. Mr. H. G. Nutt, the hon. sec. of the Lawn Tennis Club, and Captain Green carried out the admirable arrangements. Refreshments were supplied by Mr. Perry.

GENTS' SINGLES.

First round; Mr. Macnaghten beat Mr. Barry. Mr. H. Easton beat Mr. Mackenzie. Mr. Ferguson beat Mr. Davey. Mr. L. Easton beat Mr. Saltmarsh.

Second round: Mr. H. Easton beat Mr. Macnaghten, 6—1, 6—0. Mr. L. Easton beat Mr. Ferguson, 6—0, 6—1.

Final round: Mr. L. Easton beat Mr. H. Easton, 6—3, 6—2.

LADIES' DOUBLES.

First round: Miss Tomlinson and Miss Barnes beat Mrs. Carey and Miss Carey, 4—1, 4—1.

Second round: Miss Crofton and Miss E. Harding, —½15, beat Mrs. Woodfall and Miss Fardell × 15, 4—2, 5—3. Miss D. Fardell and Miss K. Fardell beat the Misses Wallis, 5—3, 4—2. Miss Barnes and Miss E. Barnes beat the Misses Sale, 4—0, 4—3. Miss Davey and Miss M. T. Sale beat Miss Tomlinson and Miss Barnes, 4—1, 4—0.

Third round: Miss Crofton and Miss E. Harding beat Miss D. and Miss F. Fardell, 4—2, 5—4. Miss Barnes and Miss E. Barnes beat Miss Davey and Miss M. T. Sale, 4—0, 4—2.

Final round: Miss Crofton and Miss E. Harding beat Miss Barnes and Miss E. Barnes, 6—4, 6—2.

LADIES' AND GENTLEMEN'S DOUBLES.

First round: Miss Fardell and Mr. Peacock, scratch, beat Mrs. Carey and Mr. L. Easton. Miss Carey and Mr. Ferguson, —15, beat Miss Powell and Mr. Mackenzie, scratch. Mrs. Woodfall and Mr. Galt, scratch. Miss Davey and Mr. Barry, scratch, byes.

Second round: Miss Fardell and Mr. Peacock beat Miss Carey and Mr. Ferguson, 7—6, 6—4. Miss Davey and Mr. Barry beat Mrs. Woodfall and Mr. Galt, 6—1, 6—2.

Final round: Miss Fardell and Mr. Peacock beat Miss Davey and Mr. Barry, 6—4, 4—6, 6—3.

GENTLEMEN'S DOUBLES.

First round: Mr. Mackenzie and Mr. Macnaghten beat Mr. Heron and Mr. Davey, 6—4, 6—7, 6—0. Mr. H. and Mr. L. J. Easton beat Mr. Peacock and Mr. Studd, 7—6, 7—6. Mr. H. Ferguson and Mr. Saltmarsh beat Mr. L. A. Hamilton and Mr. Payne.

Second round: Messrs. H. and L. J. Easton beat Mr. Ferguson and Mr. Saltmarsh, 6—1, 6—3. Mr. Mackenzie and Mr. Macnaghten, a bye.

Final round: Mr. Mackenzie and Mr. Macnaghten beat Messrs. H. and L. J. Easton, 6—4, 7—5.

Noggie came home tonight from London, to Lilian's delight. He came to call at Collingbourne straightaway, and made urgent signals that he wished to talk to Lilian alone. Steakie and I both felt we could not do other than leave them to the drawing-room together. Popped back in for my embroidery—I am sewing the dearest little cushion cover for Ruby's doll's house. Found that they were holding hands. Refrained from pointing out that Mrs Barnes might not like this sort of going-on in her house. Lilian sent me such a daggers look that I promptly succumbed and left the room again. Such was my confusion, I quite failed to pick up the wretched embroidery.

Sunday Evening
We begin to think it a little damp.

Friday 17th Oct.
The occasional appearance of a wasp enhances the many pleasures of blackberrying

Friday 10th October
We had to entertain one of the greatest bores of our acquaintance.

Had an uneasy night. A cold coming on. Affairs seem to be moving towards a crisis. Cannot but feel that Noggie is awfully young to be contemplating matrimony. Still, dearest Lilian seems to feel in control of her destiny. Wonder what it would be like to marry a younger man. Have always inclined towards men with a little more knowledge of the wider world myself—Harold Pope excepted. The responsibilities his estates have brought him contrive to make him seem far older than he is.

Fred has given Lilian a lovely diamond ring. She says they will not be married for some time. They intend waiting till Fred attains his interests. Very sensible plan. My cold much better.

Went to sit with Mollie Boucher, as Lilian is in no mood for rational conversation.
Made Scotch shortcake and had a long talk about the hundred and one things we are going to do this winter. Primary among them will be boiling up the thousands of blackberries we have collected, and making jam. Mollie declares she feels much too lazy to pick any more—her fingers are a mass of thorn sores—but I persuaded her to join me on one last blackberrying expedition before the season closes. Lilian could not be persuaded to come. She was writing to Noggie, a task she seems unaccountably to prefer to all other employments, though she saw him only yesterday. Mollie and I had more pain than

pleasure at our task. First, Captain Arbuthnot strolled by with his dog, Sandy, and would stop to chat. Then, a giant wasp erupted from the blackberry bushes and came after me in hot pursuit. Quite glad the blackberrying season is coming to a close. Cold still bad. Unable to go to Lilian's supper party to celebrate her engagement.

Still keeping indoors and finding it very SLO. Even frisking the drawing-room furniture round begins to pall. Went up and down the veranda for a change of air before dinner. The cats, Ichabod and Whitey, have been staunch comrades in my distress.

Went up the sea-wall with Lilian. She seemed very absent-minded, and did not even pretend to listen to my report of an encounter with Mrs Hatchet. I was carrying a basket of cut flowers to old Mrs Jones at the Post Office, a present from Nannie. Mrs Hatchet had the impudence to stop me in the High Street and say: 'I hope those aren't from my garden this time'. That she should still remember the incident of Frank's bouquet, shows that she has a truly un-Christian mind.

Lilian came home with me for tea. Dropped a filbert, or hazelnut, into the fire. As it chose to 'burn and die' instead of 'to crack and fly', as it ought to have done, I came to the conclusion that such practices were mere nonsense.

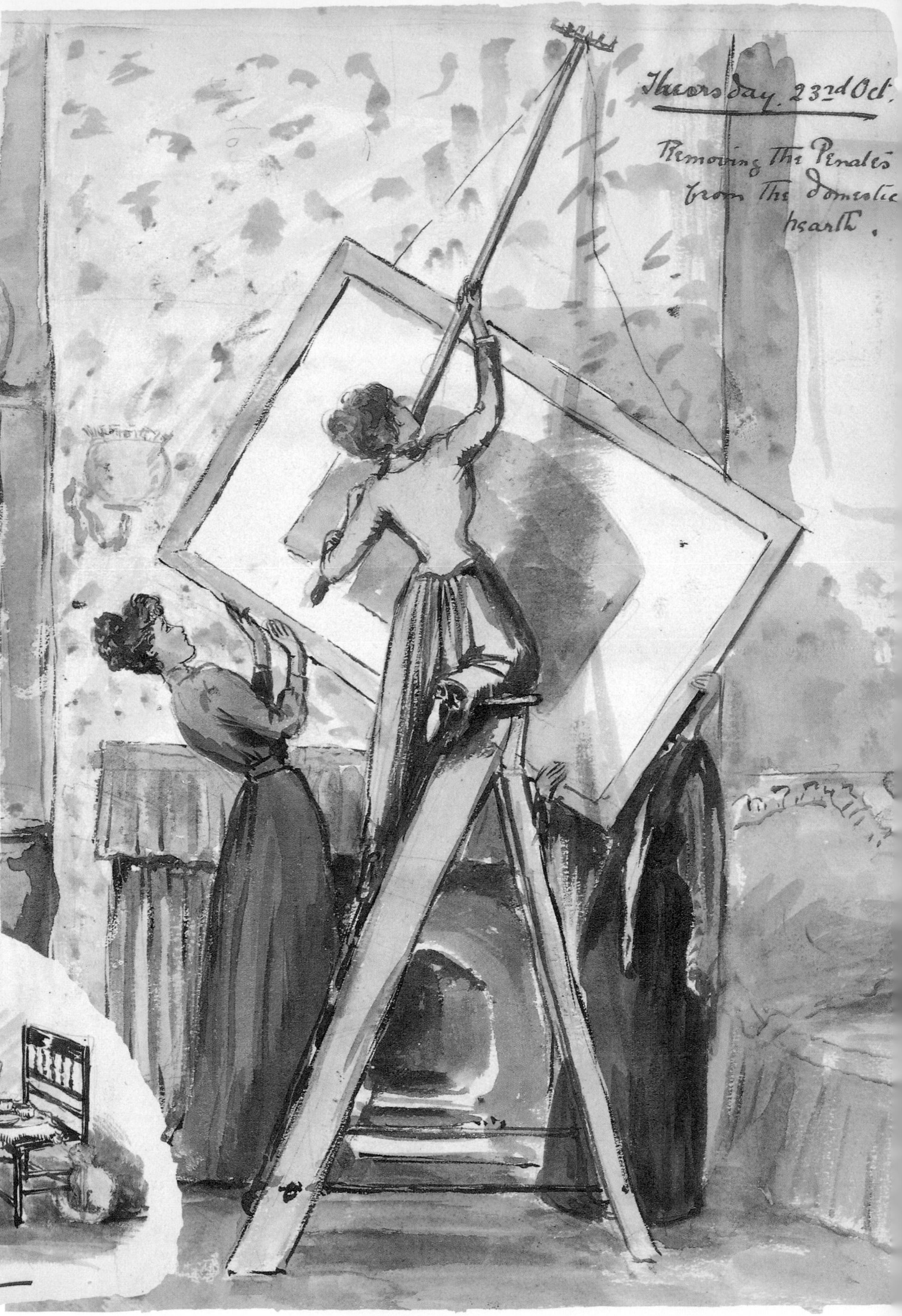

Thursday. 23rd Oct.
Removing the Penates from the domestic hearth.

Friday. 24th Oct.
"Ichabod" & "Whitey" insist on having tea with me.

November 1890

et off with Mrs Barnes to pay Mrs Hardy a visit. When nearly at her ates, remembered we did not xactly owe her a visit. None of us ould remember when she last ame to call. So we decided ɔ postpone the visit. Welcome bandonment of plan. Mrs Hardy as two Pekinese dogs which yap ıcessantly about one's ankles.

Vent over with Mollie and Mr oucher to the County Ground to atch Lilian and Steakie play in a

Thursday. 20th Nov.
In the morning we went into the Town Hall, &
found Mr Baker & Major Brown
painting some scenery — so we
assisted (?)

Curious effect of Steakie's cloak.

Thursday 12th Nov.
Emmie's mania for cultivating strange musical instruments reaches a crisis with the introduction of a "Melodion".

ırnament. Kitten Fardell was ere, looking very pretty in peach ool. Afterwards, had tea at the ouchers'. Emmie treated us to a ıne on the melodion. We begged er not to tire herself further, when e suggested playing another.

Went down to the Town Hall with Lilian. Found Major Brown and Mr Baker painting scenery for the tableaux tonight. We assisted, till they kindly told us we were more hindrance than help. Very cold weather. Fred has just come back, so Lilian is staying over at the Bouchers'. Steakie and I had a luxurious 'learn' of our parts for *The Coming Woman*. Not the same without Lilian.

Skating down by the waterworks. Luncheon on the ice. Major Brown joined us, but then left quite unexpectedly. He fell through the ice. There was the dickens of a fuss trying to get him warm and dry and home. A kind observer of the scene came to the rescue with a very doggy dog's blanket. We pummelled Major Brown till he was dry and then exhorted him to run home. Possibly the first time the Major has run in some years.

December 1890

Skating all morning, till a more than usually difficult brush with the Ice Demon led me to abandon the sport. Lilian and Mollie came here for a guitar practice.

Mrs Malden's Bible Class this morning. Tea at the von Hachts'. Guitar practice at Mollie's in the evening.

The Great G's birthday. I saved up for months to get him the treatise on the planet, Uranus, which he spied in Jervis's, the booksellers. He was delighted I could tell, although he only hurrumphed and said a birthday card would

The Buds' farewell visit, & The only Topic of real interest we could hit on was — corns.
Friday 5th Dec.

have done. Mollie's Working Party. Still sewing the child's frock I began in October. Wondered aloud if someone else would like to finish it off, so that I could start something else. Nobody volunteered. I pity the child who is given the frock.

The Bud paid a farewell visit to Collingbourne. All we could find to talk of was corns.

Met Charlie Meeres, who gave me a box of chocolates. Went with Lilian and Steakie and Georgie and Toto Jacob and Kathleen Peacock in the evening to hear a discourse on 'Love, Courtship and Marriage' at a Primitive Methodist chapel.
Very illuminating. By a happy chance, Kathleen Peacock's engagement to Willie Jacob was announced today.

Decided to make my Christmas presents this year, rather than buy them. Told Lilian of my plan, and she is determined to follow suit. We both feel that, while bought baubles are more immediately attractive, our hearts warm more to the home-made offering. Never shall I forget Aunt Bertha's quince jam. I had a stomach-ache for a week after sampling it.

Ernest Frere's ice-chair
Monday Dec. 29th.

Did think of making pots of jam for all my friends and family, but not sure how to go about it. Instead, have made little lace bags in a rainbow of colours. Mean to fill them with lavender from the garden, and tie their necks with festive ribbon.

Christmas Eve has come, but my promised treat—decorating the windows of St John's church—came to nothing. By the time I arrived, Lilian and Steakie had covered the windows in greenery till not a particle of stained glass gleamed through. Rather put out that they did not wait.

Christmas Day. Early service at Christchurch with Lilian. Morning service at St John's. Church Parade quite full. Skated with Steakie in the afternoon, and then went to Collingbourne for tea. Fred was there. I did not stay long. Mollie invited Lilian and me to supper, but I did not go. I have been most depressed all day, partly because the Christmas singers kept us awake all night. Then Nannie's cold is worse, and the Great G elected to spend Christmas in bed. He had to be entertained by relays of the family. I think I ate too much dinner, as well.

Great difficulties going to Mrs Pope's dance on Boxing Day. I was determined to go. Had not seen Harold Pope for some time. The coachman stopped half way up a hill and declared the horse, like King Wenceslas' page, could go no further. The roads were too slippery and snowbound. We got out, and, by dint of our walking up all the hills in our thin shoes, and Fred pushing the carriage while the man gee'd on the horse, we arrived at our destination. We were three hours on the road. To my great disappointment, after all that, Harold had been detained in London.

walked up the hills.

we stuck half-way.

The reflection that we saw in the glass on arriving.

Fred pushed the carriage.

Very good skating. Ernest Frere gave me a ride on his ice-chair and drove me right into another boy. He rose in the air and landed plump on top of me.

New Year's Eve. Snow fell most of the day. Colonel Jacob's party in the evening. First, we played 'Why is Somebody like Something'. Then we had supper, turkey and cranberry sauce and Guard's pudding. We played Thought-Reading till midnight. Then we waited for the clock to strike and broke our twigs and wished. Last of all, we adjourned to the dining-room, and walked round the table hand in hand, singing 'Auld Lang Syne'.

January 1891

A new year dawns, bright and frosty. Sat up till late, musing on what was to come and what had been. Read Mr Dickens's *Christmas Carol* and hoped the Ghosts of Christmastime to come would not haunt me. What will the new year bring, with what shall I fill this notebook? So mild this morning, Ethel Hargrove, Alice Neal, Douglas and Charlie Meeres and I all sat on the Prom and basked. Alice has a new muffler—very smart, a present from her mother. Charlie Meeres brought out a dancing puppet on a string and dangled it on the ground, much to the amusement of passers-by.

Skated all this morning.
Reggie Fox appeared and made us collapse with laughter, the way he dived under the legs of all the other skaters on the pond. Collapse of the stout party occurred, when Mr Meakins, the butcher, was felled like an oak by Reggie.

The Great G in a pleasant mood. Sat in his room and wrote letters all this morning as entertainment for him. In the evening played Blindman's Buff with a wooden spoon at Mrs Wilson's.

Cold bad. Stayed in bed. Nannie brought me a tisane of ambrosial honey and water. Lilian brought me old copies of *The Ladies' Pictorial*. Quiet day.

A band on the ice. The bandsme[n] looked very gay in scarlet and gold. Skated round in time to the music. Almost fell through a nasty hole.

Mrs Malden's Bible class has begun again. Went along to help her. Ruby the most eager of all th[e] children. Read to them the story

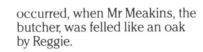

of David and Goliath. Little Toby Meakins took the story a mite too literally, and started pelting the other children with stones after the class was over.

Moonah gave one of her dancing lessons today. We all descended on her at once and she thought the best thing to do was to teach us to curtsy. Hilarious attempts at achieving the full State curtsy. Her Majesty would be delighted with our efforts.

Stormy day. Got to the end of the sea-wall. On the way, we had an argument about how to do the third step in the hornpipe. We both performed what we considered to be the right one in Fitzroy Street. Mrs Boucher was passing, on her way to the butcher's. She did stare. Practised the hornpipe further in my bedroom till the Great G banged on the wall, demanding to know if I were chasing the cat round the room.

The hornpipe has an irresistible fascination.
Tuesday Jan. 13th

Tuesday 27th Jan.
More hornpipe.

Had tea with the lodger, Bruce Chappell, who rents a cottage from Mr and Mrs Proudfoot. There was a distinct absence of tea, only a quantity of bottles of wine and slabs of Cheshire cheese. Nannie enquired whether I felt quite the thing, as I reeled home. Went to bed very early and slept late, as a result.

Short stamp down to the town today. Ordered Major Brown's guitar-ribbons. He has just taken up the instrument, and needs some encouragement in his

Saturday 24th Jan.

"The Lodger"

endeavour. Heard from Milly that she is engaged to the Lodger. He proposed when she was still recovering from the effect of much drink taken. Hope she will not regret it. Did not like to point out the evils of the path on which she has commenced. Will draw her attention to the plight of old Rufus, the tramp who was once an attorney, and now swigs whisky on the seafront.

February 1891

Bible class in the morning. Ruby is coming on very well, and now knows quite half the Old Testament. Edmund Meakins is entranced by battles, and catastrophe in general. He leapt up and down, shouting, 'Tumble down, tumble down', when I read to the children the fate of Jericho. Had Mrs Wilson, Moonah, Ethel and Ida Hargrove and Lilian and Steakie to tea. Discussed where in the world we would most like to live. Ethel chose China. The adventures of missionaries there have always thrilled her. Only the wise counsels of Ida and her mother restrained her from volunteering for service in the East, when a missionary came to Sandown to preach. Lilian chose Paris. I inclined to be satisfied with the Isle of Wight, though they all laughed at me.

Exciting news. I am to have my first painting lesson, with Mr von Hacht. The Great G was not disposed to agree to this new start of mine. Persuaded him that I would pay for it out of my running away money. Folly to miss the opportunity of learning from a live artist. Have made a special painting smock out of a pair of old brown linen curtains. Bought three painting brushes and a palette with which I hope to essay great things.

Felt very shy, arriving at Mr von Hacht's house. I am to share the cost of the lessons with a Mr Cox. Thinking a bereted figure approaching the front door must be he, I hung back till he had

ntered. Found, on my arrival, hat it had only been the butcher's boy, in point of fact. Mr Cox arrived some moments after me, his bicycle having met with a puncture. Feel I really absorbed some of the principles of painting. Mr von Hacht was so flattering as to ask me to sit for my portrait. Of the opinion that this might not be quite proper. He said I was the perfect example of the type — British spinster.

ilian and I went by the 12.30 pm rain to Freshwater. Discussed the uestion of the portrait with her n route. She advised me against itting. She did not think it quite espectable. However, as she isapproves of the whole painting nterprise, will not take her vords too much to heart.

The Meat-axe & the Minuet

Mollie and Mary Richardson were vaiting at Freshwater and we set off merrily enough for the sands. Mollie knew a shortcut by which he took us down to the shore. We scrambled about on the rocks t great risk to limbs and raiment. My boa got inextricably tangled up in a cleft in the rock. Nearly had to leave it behind. Fortunately Lilian and superior strength were at hand. She detached it from its prison without difficulty.

Visited Mrs Gibbon with Lilian and Steakie. We are all determined to have new ensembles for the summer season. *The Ladies' Pictorial* tells us that bustles are now distinctly out, and wide sleeves in fashion. Determined the summer visitors from the mainland should not put us to shame.

Friday 20th Feb.
Mollie led us down what she described as a perfectly safe & easy short cut to the shore — a most dreadful trial to my weak nerves.

riday. 20th Feb. "A long & 'appy day at Freshwater."

Could not resist having a game of football on the County Ground on the way to the tennis court. We finished abruptly as the groundsman came running up with the clear message, 'Stop desecrating my sacred turf'. Took our football, and ran.

March 1891

Dreadful storm in the night. From my little bed, I heard trees crashing and the sea roaring. Awoke late, after several hours. Snow over all the ground. Steakie feeling seedy, so only did a duty walk after tea.

Had a painting lesson, learnt the principles of perspective, attempted a sketch of Mr von Hacht. Looked to me not unlike a portrait of a coalman—my shading got a little out of control. Mr von Hacht pleased, however, and nodded till his beard shook: 'Sehr gut, Schoene'.

Walked to Ryde with Lilian—thirteen miles there and back. Enjoyable stroll, though at one point my courage failed me. We had to pass through a field full of buffaloes. Picture my distress. Lilian plucked an ashen spear from the hedgerow, and, thus armed, we passed unscathed through the danger.

"Over The hills to the "pare hauze""
Notice
This path
Monday 2nd March
The poorer we grow, the more our spirits rise.

Three lunatics bowing to the new moon.
Wednesday 11th March

Snow falling thicker than ever. Sandown as if wrapped in a fluffy blanket. Had a most exciting snowballing fight in the High Street against Mabel and Mollie.

Painting lesson in the morning. Started to draw Miss von Hacht. She made me stop, saying she was unused to being depicted like a brown cow. The similarity had not struck me before, but, once she had spoken, I saw it was very just. Mr von Hacht persuaded me to try my hand at painting a vase of anemones, instead.

Lilian and I went over to Appuldurcombe by the 5.45 pm train and stayed the night. Mrs Pope and Harold have the most distinguished manners. And the house, with its colonnades, most superior. Did not feel as shy as we expected. Mrs Pope put us quite at our ease. We sang twice with our guitars, and afterwards played 'Clumps' with the boys.

Very cold today. Oxford won the boat race, so I lost a quarter of a pound of bull's-eyes.
Painting lesson in the morning. The anemones I was painting have wilted, so started on some late primroses. Painted till the light faded. Then went for an obstacle walk on the beach, and climbed up the cliff through some most obnoxious furze bushes.

Mabel, Mollie and I and Miss Whitby went at 11.30 am to the railway bank to gather moss for church decoration. Painted till 3.30 pm, then went to Collingbourne to make tableaux dresses. Canon Whitby called after tea. The Great G and Nannie delighted to find he knew so many of their old friends.

Easter comes but once a year. Very jolly day, trumpets in the choir at morning service. Canon Whitby gave a very good sermon.

Easter Monday. Very cold. Sports in the afternoon. Little Barnaby Parrot won the egg-and-spoon by a daring leap in front of Ruby to the finishing-line. Mrs Pope's dance in the evening. Danced three times with Harold Pope, but, on the last polka, had a fearful argument with him.

May 1891

Very showery morning.
Between times, we played tennis at the Club, but there was no tea, and no one there except Bea Frere, practising her serves. She took us to Mrs Tredwell's for tea. Mrs Tredwell was a little put out by her extra guests, we thought. She drew the curtains sharply shut at 5.30 pm. We took it as a signal to depart.

Sally went off for a day out in Cowes, and returned ill.
Very worried how the parents will manage while I am at Datchet. Read to the Great G and Nannie all evening.

Sally restored to health.
Pressed on her a list of all the complaints from which the Great G suffers. Hope she can find the appropriate cure for each trouble. Instructed her not to offer him red wine, as it is undoubtedly the cause of that troublesome gout.

Left Sandown at 10.45 am, and arrived at Datchet at 3.30 pm. Delightful Red House, enchanting to be out of the Island climate. Here blossom hangs from every tree and the laburnum hedges glisten with health. Tykie gone to the races at Kempton, so I wandered about and went down to the Lodge to visit old Becky. She seems quite unchanged, still complaining about the dampness of the lodge's walls. Gave me tea and a gingerbread biscuit.

Tykie and Charlie returned and we had a grand dinner to celebrate my arrival. Charlie a little abstracted — declared he had financial worries — Tykie just as ever. Played billiards after dinner.

We went up to London in the morning. Had lunch at the Alexandra Club, Tykie and I both enjoyed it very much. Charlie went off to Pratt's. We felt we quite outdid him with our order of turkey and plum pudding. The Alexandra Club, mysteriously, seems to celebrate Christmas very early.

Wet and stormy day. Drove into Windsor to Miss Rose, the outfitter's. Ordered a new short jacket with braided lapels. It will be the envy of all Sandown. Tykie and I went for a row on the river in the afternoon. The dogs made this expedition livelier than it might have been by refusing to remain on the bank and scrambling after us into the boat.

Drove over to Slough to ask Daisy Green, an old girl from Miss Kirby's in York, to lunch on Tuesday. Mrs Green still invalid, received us lying back on a sofa covered in green chintz. She did not at all relish the idea of Daisy coming over, but, as we offered to fetch and return her, she could think of no other objection.

The Duke sent me a badge for Kempton races, but it was too wet to go.

M.J. Don't you think it wrinkles a little in the back!
But you will not frequently stand in that position, madam.

Datchet. May.
"Whene'er we take our walks abroad"?

Thursday 14th May
Datchet
Moral: If people tell you that
Their dogs will be content to run along
the bank while you are in a boat
Do not believe them!!!!

Princess Christian opened the Datchet Art Exhibition today. She looked very pretty, wrapped up against the chill air with a large muff. They say she has never recovered properly from the birth of her child. Rained all the afternoon, did some dressmaking. Tykie provided a pattern which would do equally well for both of our sizes, she said. The resulting skirt, however, did not do justice to either of us.

Wrote home for leave to stay here till Ascot Week. Tykie has promised to take me.
Small chance I might see the Duke.

Played billiards as usual in the evening. Dreadful accident. Charlie Cooper, who came to lunch, fell over and brought down with him the lamp and most of the billiard cues. We joked he was *Hari-kari*-ing on.

another miss!!
Datchet. May. Our principal occupation.

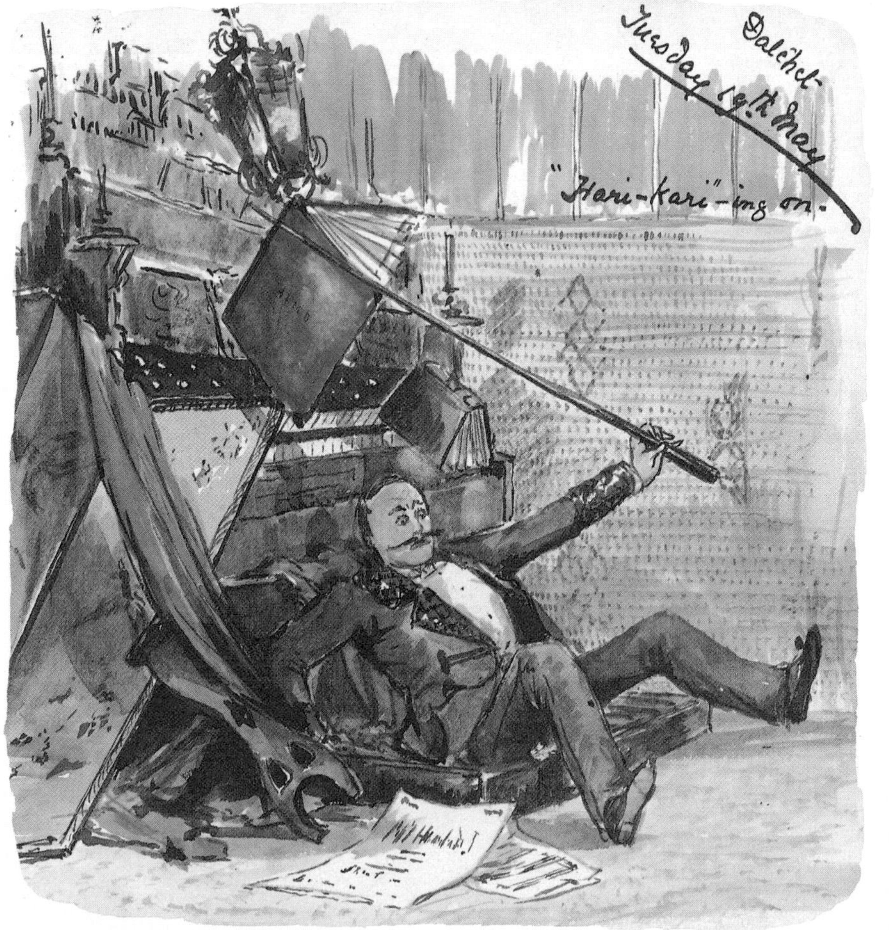
Datchet
Tuesday 19th May
"Hari-kari"-ing on.

June 1891

Charlie and Toddie are going to stay at the Savoy for several days. Very envious, suggested they might relish some company in town. Very willing to go with them. Tods said it was a sweet offer, but they would be very busy, and she thought it best for me to remain here. Fed the dogs, and sketched in the punt most of the afternoon.

Read all about the Tranby Croft affair. Sir William Cummings, playing Baccarat with the Prince of Wales, cheated. When the news leaked out, he brought a court case. The Sovereign, who disapproves of gambling, is said to be shaken to the core. Wonder if I should give up my games of whist.

My usual Luncheon party.
Thorpe June.

Mr Ritchie, a friend of Charlie's from the Colonies, arrived to stay unexpectedly so I have the interesting role of being both host and guest. We drove round the countryside in the phaeton. Mr Ritchie told me much about sugar in Malaya which I conscientiously absorbed.

Took all the dogs for a walk. Chummie, Dinah and Jack all very frisky without Charlie's usual exercise. Took them down by the river and had forcibly to restrain Chummie from dragging us all into the briny.

News from abroad. I can stay for Ascot, and the Great G has sent me half a crown with which to back a horse of my choosing.

A bad start.

I rashly took all the dogs (including dear Harry) out for a walk

ecked out my hat with ribbons, ıd persuaded Toddie to do ıe same.

harlie and Toddie and I had a ɔecial lunch before going off to scot, with shrimps and ıampagne. Lovely day, onderful scenes with hundreds people in top hats and striped esses, gay against the green of e Turf. Met Charlie Cooper, to y surprise. He took me up to the p of the stand to see one race won by a horse called Merrilees. I had put all the Great G's half a crown on it, so I was mighty pleased.

Ascot each day. Wore my black and mauve stripe on Tuesday; Wednesday, my yellow and white dress. Mr Ritchie stood us all lunch in a tent. Very crowded. A lady of fifty in a feathered hat and black bombazine collapsed from the heat, and was carried most dramatically from her table.

Distinctly saw the Duke of Clarence pass on his way to the Royal Box. Most excited.

Ascot Week and dissipation at an end, I took the dogs for a walk. Will miss them when I go, but the Great G will never allow me to keep a pet. His heart is wedded to the memory of Frederick, the fox terrier he had in York. Walked as far as Penton Hook Lock to watch the boats come up the river. Had champagne for dinner, as it was my last night.

Took Chummie for a final walk round the garden. Then left Egham for home, and reached Sandown in the evening. Just too late to go with the others to Mr Wise's farewell dinner, so they had to sit down thirteen to dinner.

Very nice to be home. The whole summer stretches peacefully ahead. Had my first painting lesson of the season. Painted some gladioli. Difficult to get the salmon colour exactly. Had a great excitement this evening. Wilfred Parker gave me a ride on the front of his tricycle. Very frightening experience. Doubt if I shall repeat it. Steakie has declared her intention to purchase a bicycle for herself, and she means to wear divided skirts to ride it. Very much afraid she still nurses dreams of becoming a New Woman.

July and August 1891

Painting class in the morning. Drew Miss von Hacht's portrait. Alarming report that the dancing bear has killed its keeper and got loose without a muzzle. Imagined what havoc it would create in the High Street, lumbering into every shop.

Lilian went off today to London. Went down to the station to see her off. Only the sturdy presence of Mr Porteus, the station master, prevented me from bursting into tears. We saw her off with a gaiety that was close to tears. Had two sets afterwards, to try and dispel the gloom.

Played a lot of tennis this month, and did the Clothing Club—usually with Steakie. Mrs Jenkins's dispute over her children's dresses still looms large.

Attempted Mollie's portrait. She is a very fidgety subject, and would not keep still. Eventually, abandoned the attempt to immortalize her features and began drawing her dog.

Called on the Beauchamp-Peacocks with Nannie. Much admired their new tea-service, blue with a gold Greek cross motif.

Moths!
Friday 17th July
I began to reap the
of having invested
a shrimping

Saturday
Began Mollie's portrait, but progressed slowly, on account of the occasional total eclipse of my model.

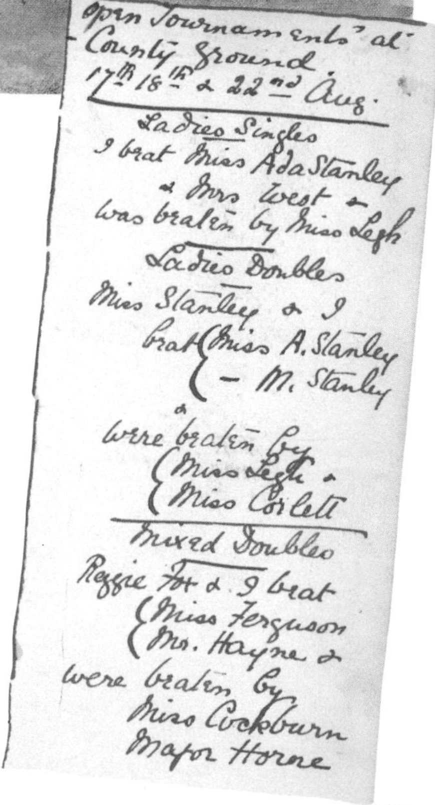

ugust

ally went off on the spree today, nd once more returned home ill. osed her with Dr Collis Brown's nixture, but secretly thought ere was nothing wrong with her at a teetotal day would not cure.

Made a lot of calls today. Called on Mrs Beauchamp-Peacock again, more for the pleasure of seeing her tea-service than for any other reason. Her drawing-room is sumptuous, with linen antimacassars and deep blue velvet curtains. Lilian told me in confidence that Mrs Beauchamp-Peacock has three silk petticoats. How she made this discovery I know not, but feel deeply envious. Wonder if this is every married woman's lot. Nannie wears flannel next to the skin, I know.

Played tennis at the Club with Herbert Peacock, Steakie and Lilian. Herbert sported a very beautiful red and white cummerbund, but, nevertheless, we lost two sets.

Among the visitors who have come to the Island for their holidays are Colonel and Miss Lily Berkeley. They last came two years ago. Colonel Berkeley now seems to be recovering well from the sad death of his wife, Anna Sophia. Such a distinguished man, and so indulgent of his daughter, Lily. He gave Lilian and me a huge box of chocolates each. Placed the ribbon from my box under my pillow. Felt it would bring me good luck. Did not mention this to Colonel Berkeley when I met him this morning on the esplanade. He looked immensely trim, his moustaches as military as his bearing. He kindly turned back with me, and, without any prompting, offered to buy me an ice at Doré's. Not sure whether to make anything of this.

19th Aug: Wednesday
My partner proves to be
rather a trial for weak
nerves.

Thursday. 26th Aug.
A fair sample of August weather in 1891

What the most enthusiastic tennis-players
were reduced to "Tip and Shy" Aug. 31st Monda

When we told fortunes at Mollie's this afternoon, mine read: 'What you have now, protect and cherish.'

Lily Berkeley came to tea. Such lovely fair hair. Believe she takes after her mother, as the Colonel's hair is almost red. She hinted that the Colonel had been asking after me. As he only saw me yesterday, feel this is a hopeful sign. Strange the bond I feel with them both, though their Indian experiences give them a sophistication to which I cannot aspire. Must enquire if he knew General Gordon. Or perhaps that was China?

Lily came to tea again. Nannie very amused by her tales of life in India. She was there with her father till the last years of his exile in the Army there. She brought with her a huge box of chocolates, a present from Colonel Berkeley. Sent home with her a note of thanks, on writing-paper suffused with the scent of Parma violets.

Shanklin
Cinderella Dance
Friday Aug. 21st.

1 Valse H. Pope
2 Valse Sycamore
3 Polka Ernest Frere
4 Valse Naggie
5 Valse S. Hillier
6 Valse Frank Boucher
7 Lancers Mr. Ford
8 Valse Sycamore
9 Valse W. F. Fisher
10 Polka W. F. Fisher
11 Valse Frank Boucher
12 Valse S. Hillier
13 Valse H. Pope
14 Lancers H. R. Hewett
15 Valse Ernest Frere
16 Valse H. Pope
17 Valse H. Pope
18 Polka Ernest Frere

Shanklin Cinderella.
Friday. 28th Aug.

1 Valse Shepherd
2 Valse Woodthorpe.
3 Polka W. F. Fisher
4 Valse Naggie
5 Valse S. Hillier.
6 Valse Harold Pope
7 Lancers Johnnie Sinclair
8 Valse Ernest Frere
9 Valse J. Sinclair
10 Polka Reggie Fox
11 Valse S. Hillier
12 Valse Harold Pope
13 Valse Fred. Fox
14 Lancers Woodthorpe
15 Valse Harold Pope
16 Valse Ernest Frere
17 Valse Harold Pope
18 Polka Ernest Frere
Extras.
1 Waltz Fred. Fox
2 Galop Ernest Frere
3 Waltz Shepherd.

Friday 28th Aug.
My partner (J.S.) objects to being subjected to the same treatment as the floor i.e. covered with French Chalk

Club tournament. With my usual luck, I was out in the first round. However as Colonel Berkeley told me when commiserating, the best man does not always win. Since I have never won, felt cheered by this remark. Watched Lilian and Fred swoop to victory with a cheerful heart.

Colonel Berkeley brought me a huge box of chocolates.

Club tournament third round. Rain stopped play at 12 pm, so retreated to the Collingbourne library. Wrote letters and played cards till 5 pm when we were too bored to remain any longer. Put on mackintoshes and braved the rain. Met Colonel Berkeley and Lily, also out for a wet stroll. They came back to Collingbourne and toasted teacakes on a griddle. Lovely day.

September to December 1891

Many of the summer visitors have gone, but the Berkeleys remain. Colonel Berkeley is to take me to the Glee concert this evening. He has been so long out of England, that he was quite astonished when I mentioned this beloved form of entertainment. Delighted to find he is so partial to music.

Went with Steakie to a Missionary Meeting in the Stanleys' garden. Very hot day, and the missionaries spoke for too long. Pledged ten shillings from my Christmas money for our black brothers.

Took our guitars down to the Drabbles. Arthur out shooting with Harold Pope, so only Mrs Drabble an audience for the 'Venetian Boat Song' and 'Wait till de sun am hot'. Mrs Pope's dance in the evening. None of us wanted to go. Tired of dances. The men were weary after shooting. All in all, not the jolliest of occasions. Danced with Harold Pope twice, Colonel Berkeley did not come.

17th September 1891. I am in heaven. Colonel Berkeley confided to me that he feels the responsibility of his daughters gravely. Apologized for bothering me. Only too pleased to help.

Saturday, 19th September. More than ever in heaven. JCB came about seven, and stayed till half-past. He talked of the difficulties a widower faces in the world. Nannie suspects nothing.

JCB took us all into Ryde, and we had tea at Marlow's.

Putting ourselves & the conflagration out. Friday. Sept. 25th

JCB came to interview the parents. The Great G very upset at first, when I told him the news. Wondered aloud who now would read to him in the evenings. Lilian tells me Mr Barnes had much the same reaction to her declaration. The Great G relieved to know JCB is a military man.

After the fateful interview when the Colonel asked for my hand in marriage, we went down to the Arcade to join the others. Celebrated the approaching nuptials with lashings of tea. Feels very strange to think I shall soon be Lily's step-mamma. Nervous of the responsibility but, with Jim's help, I shall cope.

October

JCB called to say goodbye to the parents.

JCB and Lily left today. Went down to the station to see them off, against the Great G's wishes. Mr Porteus was, thank goodness, busy chatting to the guard when Colonel Berkeley kissed me. He promised to write from London. Came away, feeling miserable.

Letter from Colonel Berkeley, desiring me to come to London and meet his relations. Thrilled with the idea. Nothing like a spree in London. Nannie very agitated—needlessly, I told her. She thinks Sir George Berkeley and Sir James and Lady Peile much too grand for the likes of me. Reminded her that I often met Lady Langrishe at Tykie's.

Went down to the Prom with Lilian. Had a most enlightening talk about our futures. Lilian vowed she would follow Fred wherever he chose to go. Only hoped it would not be Malaya, as she could not fancy the climate. Relieved to think Colonel Berkeley is now resident in London for good and aye. Wrote my reply to his letter in the afternoon.

Another sweet letter by today's post. Very eager for me to follow him to London. Broached the subject to Nannie and the Great G. They agreed, if reluctantly. Wrote back: 'Yes' this afternoon.

Letter from JCB, and a lovely pair of gloves. Wore them all about the house, till the Great G asked if I was getting too finickety to bare my arms. Showed them to Lilian, who was also a trifle disparaging. Did not like to ask her if Fred had given her any such tokens.

Lilian and I had a long stamp on the sea-wall and discussed serious things. In particular, we taxed our brains with the question of economical housekeeping. Wish I had taken more account of the weekly bills

6th Oct. Tuesday.
A suitable day for doing the Pier.

ıe tradesmen furnish, rather ıan just paying them. Asked 'annie what were the most nportant elements in ousekeeping. She said, keeping ıe servants in order, and buying nly the best sago.

pent ages deciding what to pack ɔr the visit. Sir George Berkeley nd Sir James Peile sound so very rand, my usual outfit of blouse nd skirt seems inappropriate. 'ent to Mrs Gibbon for advice. he is constructing even now a ɔstume with enormous sleeves. o idea how I will be able to eat r drink without trailing my eeves in my plate. What we omen endure for the sake of shion. Bought two new ght-gowns, one edged with pink bbon, one with blue. Another veet letter. Felt so exhilarated, ad another long stamp on the a-wall.

November

Lilian and Steakie loyally saw me on my way over to Portsmouth. Felt very excited, while with them. Lilian joked that I was going to get married secretly in London, and surprise them all. Spirits rather fell during the train journey. I shared my compartment with an elderly lady and a parrot. The parrot would sing out 'Good morning, *bonjour'*, and the elderly lady would reply 'Good morning to you' till my nerves could barely stand it. Thrilled and relieved to see Jim standing, at his most military and erect, on Victoria Station. London feels very grimy after Sandown. Staying with Tykie in a very nice hotel in Phillimore Gardens.

Had dinner at Hyde Park Mansions with Sir George Berkeley, Jim's brother. Much admired the tusks mounted in silver on the wall. Sir George told me they were the sad remains of a favourite elephant on which he used to ride in West Africa. Was questioned carefully about my family over the mutton. Proudly told of the Great G's years at St Peter's, and of Herbert's position at London University. Jim beamed, so that seemed to be all right. Sir George's housekeeper, Miss Birtwhistle, enquired of me, over some weak tea, whether I was accustomed to running a home. I must come to her for any tips I might need, she said. Very grateful, but doubt if I will do so. Have run Fernside for many a year. Looking forward to trying my hand in London.

Dinner with Sir James and Lady Peile, Jim's sister and brother-in-law, in Campden Hill Court. They have a most commodious flat in the building, and all the walls are covered in delicate watercolour sketches of monkeys in the jungle. The Peiles were stationed in Bombay, and have their mementoes, too—tusks, brass bowls and elephant foot umbrella stands. Vowed secretly never to allow Jim to hang a single tusk in our home. Lady Peile rather an invalid—a dreamy face hidden among swathes of lace. She enquired after the parents, and promised me some gooseberry jelly for Nannie but forgot it as soon as she proposed it.

Jim took me to the Royal Academy, where I much admired several pictures. Afterwards we repaired to Messrs Fortnum and Mason's establishment. Had seed cake and an American dish called muffins for tea. Truly happy.

JCB took Ethel, Mrs Lyde, his married daughter who lives in India, and me to St James's Theatre. Enjoyed the play greatly. Afterwards went to the Junior Army and Navy Club for tea. Much enjoying my rackety time.

Dined again with Sir George Berkeley. Find his flat quite oppressive, secretly. Suppose he grew used to living in dark and dank quarters in the West Indies. The white lace of the tablecloth the only bright spot in the room.

All duty visits now done, returned to Sandown to the bosom of my family. Passed through Datchet on my way. Wept copiously when Tykie and Beatrice and Kiddah gathered for a last evening with me before the nuptials. Thought of all the jolly ideas we had for next summer, when we were going to go to Germany. Now perhaps I will go with Jim. Reading the volume of *Tennyson's Works* which he gave me.

December

Home for the very last time. Spent most of the day unpacking, then read to the Great G and Nannie. Both very eager to hear how the Visit went. Reassured them that both Sir George Berkeley and Lady Peile made me most welcome.

So many things to discuss, so many things to arrange. Packing up a lifetime between sheets of tissue paper. It will be a very quiet wedding, naturally, as it is Jim's second attempt. Determined, none the less, to have a hat of some magnificence, such as has never been seen in Sandown before. Combed the pages of *The Ladies' Pictorial*, and found just what I wanted—a grey silk hat with ostrich plumes. Mrs Gibbon is to copy it.

Between preparations for Christmas and correspondence with Jim and organizing the wedding, feel quite dizzy. Lilian has been a brick, helping me to choose capes and coats and skirts for my New Life. Sad that her own Happy Time will not come for some years.

Spent all afternoon cutting an old lace frock into bits, with which to adorn Christmas cards. Told fortunes afterwards. Mine came out: 'He who loses his all will surely recover it likewise'. Mystified as to the meaning of this. Puzzled over it for quite some hours.

It was so cold & draughty at the Cricket match
that we were obliged to shelter behind
the Pavilion where we could
see nothing.

Settling in London

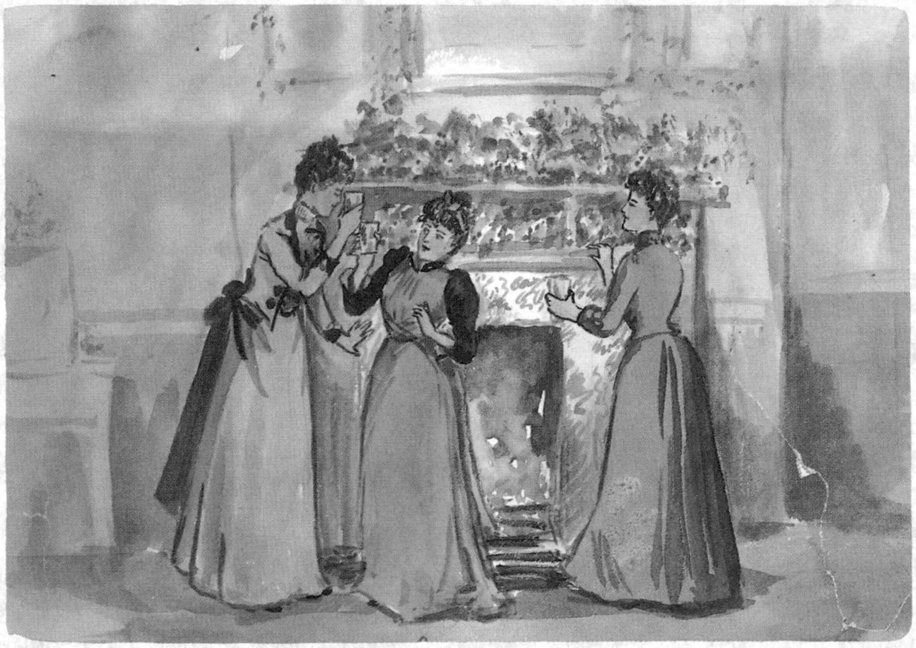

1892 to 1895

January to March 1892

Thursday 21st January

"The trembling bride"

Never really thought I would be first, of Lilian and me, to grace the altar of Christchurch in a wedding veil. This day, Thursday, 21st January 1892, I waited, with Mr Boucher at my side, for dear Jim to come up the aisle. I wore heavy silk poplin lined with crisp taffeta, and I got Mrs Gibbon to tag silver flounces all round the hem and the neckline to the great advantage of the dress. I carried white chrysanthemums and my hat was trimmed with some birds' feathers Shoggie found in the wood. I really felt I looked my best for Jim. (The girls and I had wild hoots of laughter, trying to get ready at Fernside. Lilian wore mauve, and Steakie pink and black.) Owing to all the rumpus, neither the Great G nor Nannie were present at the ceremony. The Great G gave me a set of Milton, and Nannie a comb-case, to mark my nuptials.

It was very quiet, and Jim and I exchanged our vows very simply and solemnly. Could not help but feel glad that none of Jim's daughters had come. Would have looked very strange, a bride of thirty-two and daughters not much younger. We put chrysanthemums all round the altar and at the back of the church, so there was a very festive air to the proceedings. Unfortunately, Jim, whose eyesight is not perfect after those long years under the Indian sun, failed to see the stand of chrysanthemums at the back, such was his haste to reach the front of the church. Lilian told me it teetered alarmingly, before deciding to settle in place. Jim looked splendid, in a grey flannel coat and with a carnation in his buttonhole—more imposing than I had ever seen him.

The ceremony did not pass without another hitch. While Noggie was kneeling by Jim, ready to hand him the ring, his left leg inadvertently slipped out behind him, and he sent both his and Jim's top hats for six.

Jan. 21st The bridal procession to the Station

The vicar and I exchanged glances of dismay, but Lilian sprang out of her pew, dusted the offending items off and restored them to their owners. Peace restored, the ceremony went ahead. We had tremendous fun in the vestry after Jim had tenderly pressed the ring on to my finger and the ceremony was complete. Everyone insisted on coming in. We had difficulty in getting the register signed at all, especially as Shoggie suddenly had the bright idea of hiding it from view, which confused us all considerably.

The entire party—Lilian, Steakie, Shoggie, Noggie, Uncle Ward and Mr Boucher—accompanied us down to the station where Mr Porteus was kind enough to present me with a bouquet in honour of the day. As the train

Ventnor. The kind of weather we enjoyed on the honeymoon

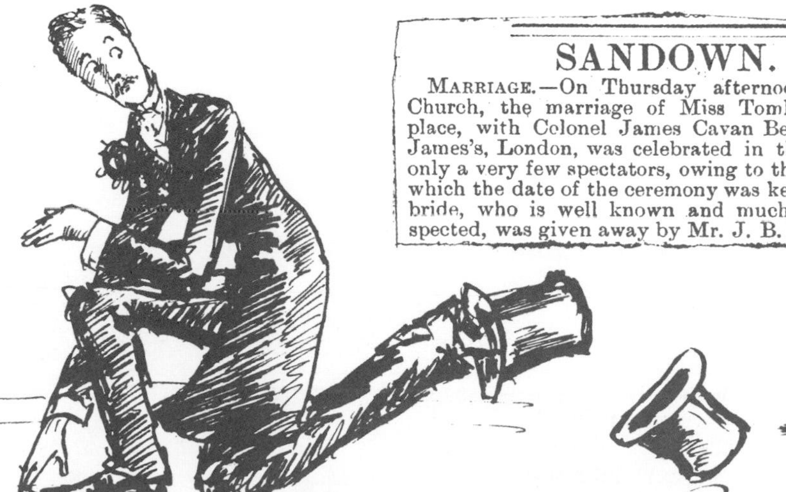

The only part which the "Best Man" took in the ceremony.

SANDOWN.

MARRIAGE.—On Thursday afternoon, at Christ Church, the marriage of Miss Tomlinson, of this place, with Colonel James Cavan Berkeley, of St. James's, London, was celebrated in the presence of only a very few spectators, owing to the success with which the date of the ceremony was kept secret. The bride, who is well known and much liked and respected, was given away by Mr. J. B. Boucher.

vas late, Jim had good
pportunity to hear much of my
ast exploits at the station from
Ir Porteus. I was quite put to
ne blush.

im has decided on Ventnor as a
uitable place for our
oneymoon. Cannot help but
vonder where he took Anna
ophia. Determined not to let her
oor departed name be a bone of
ontention between us. Would
ot be at all surprised to hear it
vas Paris, however. In his
ounger days, I gather, the
olonel cut a very dashing figure.

Ve go for a great many
onstitutionals, though the
eather is unremittingly bad.
uggested we telegram to Lilian
nd Steakie and ask them to visit
s one day. Surprised to find dear
m quite adamant that they
hould not. He takes the nature of
honeymoon rather more
eriously than do I. I thought it
ould be fun to give the girls a
eat. And they would certainly
ven up the Bonchurch Hotel.
here is a particular soda syphon
n the sideboard in the dour
ining-room here which simply
ries out to be used in some
iece of horseplay. The Colonel, I could see, was not amused when I mentioned this. It seems that married ladies do not behave with that lack of circumspection on which Lilian and Steakie and I had always prided ourselves.

Scene at Victoria
Feb. 3rd
Wednesday
I think this must be mine (?) but I can't see the label
M.B.
a few of the bride's baubles.

Returned to Sandown. The Great G and I had a tearful farewell in the library. He pressed a copy of Keats's poems, which he used to read with the boys at St Peter's, on me, saying that, now I was a married lady, it was suitable for me to read such verse. Feel most touched by his thoughtfulness.

February

Lady Peile came to call, bringing with her a jar of quince jelly. She surprised us all. We were practising our guitars when she arrived, and having great fun. In the nicest possible way, she made us feel slatterns. She asked all sorts of difficult questions about the gas lamps and about my Domestic Economy. Mindful of the lavish entertaining at Campden Hill Court, I bade The Cook produce teacakes and muffins for tea. Imagine my horror when an enormous gateau appeared . Lady Peile's eyebrows shot up to her forehead under her veil. What she thought of such extravagance, I do not know. Lily and Trixie did not help matters by exclaiming with delight, and protesting that I spoilt them. Lady Peile will think I was putting on 'side', Anna Sophia would never have allowed such a thing to happen. After tea, Lady Peile demanded a complete tour of the house. She approved of her nieces' rooms, plainly furnished with truckle beds and flowered curtains. Could see she thought my bedroom an unwanted piece of vanity. She lifted up the frill around my dressing-table, explaining she was curious to know what defect it hid. Relieved our feelings, once she had gone, with a resounding chorus on the guitars.

Lily, Trixie, Ethel and I having tremendous larks organizing the new home. Sated my desire for the Japanese, hanging fans and parasols above the mantelpiece in the drawing-room. Wanted to

"Tuning up"

On the stairs
In the drawing-room

"Patience" broke out on Thursday 18th Feb. & has raged with great virulence ever since.

place a few spare ones in Jim's library, but he refused this treat. Embroidering him a pair of slippers with the motif of golden keys crossed over the toes. The keys to my heart, I romantically informed him, but I don't think he heard.

Had great fun playing Patience in the last few days. Jim came home in the middle of one intense bout of it, and seemed rather put out that I was not more pleased to see him. Unfortunately, so deeply involved in the game was I that I had quite forgotten to order dinner. Jim retired to his club.

Lily decided to test out the efficiency of the speaking-tube between the drawing-room and kitchen. She retreated to the latter, and trumpeted down the tube. I was nearly blown away with the force of it.

Helped her wash her hair this evening. Such lovely long golden hair. Unfortunately, the water with which I doused her was nearer hot than tepid, and she squawked like a chicken.

March

The fancy has taken us to have a Turkish bath. Ethel was first recommended to take this unusual type of exercise by her doctor in India, when she complained of lassitude. Apparently, it invigorates the cells of the skin and promotes well-being. We decided we were all in need of this aid to health.

Very charming baths, tiled in turquoise. Expected a Turkish pasha to leap out at any moment and entice us into his harem. Ethel poured scorn on these fancies.

Felt very strange and defenceless wrapped in towels. Remembered Jim's words, that the whole event promotes spiritual as well as physical well-being. Tried to feel spiritual, but only succeeded in feeling first very hot, in the steaming room, and then very sticky in the tepidarium. Hoped that the attendant might bring us Turkish sweetmeats as we lay on our couches, but she only brought more and more towels.

Lee Lee gives me a blow (up the speaking-tube)

Trixie regrets having offered to carry home the cake.

Saturday. 20th Feb.

I helped Lily to wash her hair (A slight coolness between us for some time afterwards) The water was perhaps rather warm!

Wednesday. 30th March

A bootless expediti

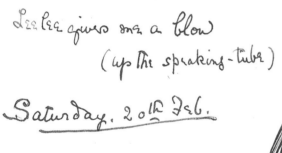

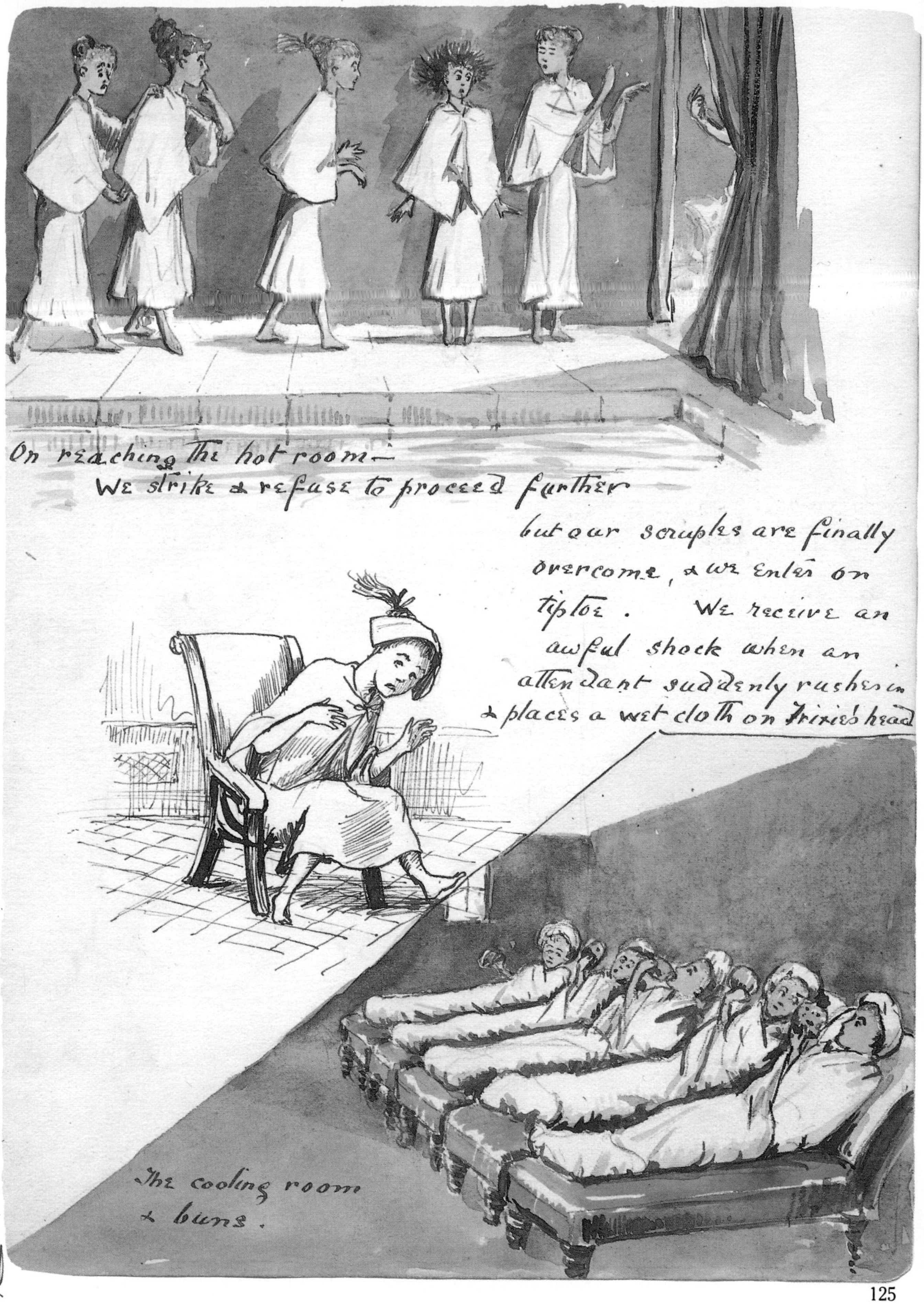
On reaching the hot room—
We strike & refuse to proceed further
but our scruples are finally overcome, & we enter on tiptoe. We receive an awful shock when an attendant suddenly rushes in & places a wet cloth on Trixie's head
The cooling room & buns.

April and August 1892

Our visit to The Zoo. April.
"Hello"!

Jim took us all to the Zoo today. Wore my new hat, trimmed with primroses from the park. Lily and Trixie put roses in their hair. How people did stare. Enjoyed the day very much, though did not care to see the animals caged. A very mangy lion was evidently longing to be back in the wilds of Kenya. As for a parrot which jumped off its perch to attack me and caw 'Hello', I would be very glad to see it safely back in Africa. Expected Long John Silver to come round the corner at any moment.

Had a great deal of difficulty at home with the new invention which attaches to the bathroom taps. It is intended to give one what is called a shower bath. When I attempted to take one of these new-fangled things, the hose leapt out of the bath and turned itself on me. Decidedly prefer the old way of bathing in a hip bath.

My first attempt to use the new invention for the hot-water was not a success.

August

Lovely to be at Sandown again, if not at the parents' home. We would not all fit, so Jim has taken rooms in the Pier Hotel. Always my ambition to stay here. Lily, Ethel and Trixie know it of old, of course. The Great G and Nannie seem somehow to have shrunk, in the short time since I last saw them. Very difficult now to get Nannie to come for an airing on the Prom.

The immoral game of croquet. We played at 'Los Altos', Lilian and Steakie joined us there. Lilian and I got ahead of the field by a series of dexterous strokes. I just managed to push my croquet mallet against the ball, which just managed to squeeze through the hoop, while nobody was looking. Felt very wicked afterwards. Repented in my evening prayers.

Took the 'bus over to Shanklin for the Bachelors' Dance, all wrapped up for fear of spoiling our dresses. Was somewhat astonished at the deference with which Wilfrid Parker and Charlie Meeres and many others treated me. Was not asked to dance overmuch, though I had one *valse* with Harold Pope for old times' sake. Wish Jim could be here, to see me—an elegant swan with pink plumage.

Played cricket on the sands, an entertainment new to Sandown since I lived here. Little Ruby Barnes was an excellent fielder, she has really come on since I left Sandown. Noggie has been giving her lessons, she confided. The only fly in the ointment was that poor Lily, striving to catch a ball, fell over a lobster pot and cricked her ankle.

Cricket on the sands.
A graceful catch.

A disputed point.
Sandown. Aug. 1892.

Sandown. Aug. 1892. We find the glare of the new Esplanade necessitates the use of blue glasses.

The result of Uncle Gruffie's pet stroke
...nis Club. Aug. 1892.

Shanklin Bachelors' Dance 27 Aug. 1892

Steakie would not allow anyone to enter the 'bus till she had carefully explained that there were 10 of us, that the 'bus only held 8, and that we were already very late.

Immense drama today. Ethel and Trixie put out to sea in a canoe, determined to brave the ocean wave. Hardly had they got out of the cover of friendly Sandown Bay before a commotion in the water convinced them that all was not well. Next moment, they saw a shiny black fin knifing its way through the water. It was a shark of immense proportions. Ethel, being interested in natural history, was keen to catch it with an old fishing line in the boat. Trixie, thankfully, saw sense and insisted they turn for home. Not sure whether to tell their father of this. Feel it reflects poorly on me, the guardian in whom he has placed his trust.

Ethel & Trixie put to sea in a canoe and meet a shark.

November and December 1892

Nice to be home again, though there is all the unpacking to be done. Very glad to see Jim once more, and hear all the news. He has spent much of his time at his Club.

Trixie has gone mad over card tricks, and makes our lives a burden with her demands for attention. Lily and I escaped to the sanctuary of the bathroom today, where we washed all the plants. The aspidistra has got caked in dust since we have been away, and the ferns are no better. Got almost as wet as the plants, washing them. Joyful task, restoring order to chaos. Distributed the plants in quite different corners of the house. Positioned the Swiss cheese plant rather awkwardly between the umbrella stand and the front door. Jim mistook it in the darkness last night for the umbrella stand and knifed through the leaves with his walking stick. Fear it can never be the same again.

Jim took us all to the pantomime today. Came back late. In my bedroom when I suddenly heard strange noises coming from my wardrobe. Did not dare to investigate on my own. Knew Jim would dismiss my fears as fancies. Called Lily and Trixie to my room and debated what to do. Sure there was a robber concealed within the wardrobe. Imagined him with his crowbar and jemmy, ready to spring. Lily whispered that the servants had heard rumours that a burglar was working in the area. Might have stood there all night, only Lily took matters into her capable hands. She seized a parasol by its handle and advanced on the wardrobe saying very firmly, 'Come out before I poke out your eyes with my parasol.' Then she opened the wardrobe door. Our hearts were in our mouths. Thank goodness, there was nothing inside but my new grey slub silk dress. Jim thought us all very silly when he heard of our adventure.

He was confirmed in this opinion of our idiocy when he came home to find us all pressed against the drawing-room wall. We had just come down, changed for dinner, when the most entrancing music began to float through the wall between us and the next house. The best way to hear it was to lean against the wall and listen. A string quartet was playing. Dreamt I lived in marble halls and had concerts at whim. Very much hope these musicians have taken the house for good. Had dinner to the soft accompaniment of Schubert from next door.

Trixie: "Choose any card"!!

London. Nov. 1892.

Trixie has gone mad over card-tricks, & makes our lives a burden

Washing the plants in the bath.

Looking in my wardrobe for robbers. Sunday. Nov. 1892

December

Our first Christmas together. Hardly seems possible that a year has flown by so quickly. Canvassed the opinions of all the girls. They all agreed that it was indeed a miracle. Jim's only complaint concerned the quality and dullness of the cooking. He enjoys spicy food.

Decided the home was a happy one, both Lily and Trixie are pleased to live with us. And the staff is happy enough below stairs. Nevertheless, took Jim's strictures on the number of times we have eaten cold lamb with peas seriously. Will ask Cook to try for a little more variety in her menus.

The arrival of Xmas Cards is a great excitement. The whole household continually meet round The letter-box.

Ethel's fireworks. 5th Nov. 1892 London.

Dec. 1892.

February 1893

Trixie & I invariably lose our shuttlecock in the gas.

Very exciting addition to the household in the shape of one poorly trained mongrel. Lily found him slavering over some old bits of newspaper in the Square Gardens. Rather taken aback, when she brought him home, and insisted we hang a notice on the area steps announcing 'One lost dog found'. Nobody has claimed him yet, however, so we have named him 'Pat' and spend every waking hour trying to train him to be good. The General (as Jim now is!) says it is a hopeless task, but we persevere. Pat has a way of looking up at one with his brown eyes that makes one's heart turn over. He has his livelier moments, too. When we were playing battledore and shuttlecock in the drawing-room last week, Pat worried at the shuttlecock every time it landed near him. 'Good dog', we had to say, and only then would he release it.

We all got so expert that we practised playing with our left hands and with two shuttlecocks.

Still busy decorating the house. So satisfying to have a home of my own, at last. Cannot go to any great expense, however, as we only have the lease of Kensington Gardens for six months.
Bought a lot of silver to supplement Jim's stock, as well as toast racks and tantaluses and salt cellars of which one can never have enough. Fortunate, I suppose, to have all the china Anna Sophia brought as her dowry. Would have preferred a fresh start, though would not dream of upsetting Jim and the girls by saying so.

The painting mania,
Lily's portrait.
Feb. 1893.

At one time we were all at work on Lily's portrait, Trixie was painting some of the background, while I struggled with the nose, — and the "model" walked round us with a bottle of "turps" and rubbed superfluous paint off our garments with a rag.

Feb. 1893.

91 Kensington Gardens Square.

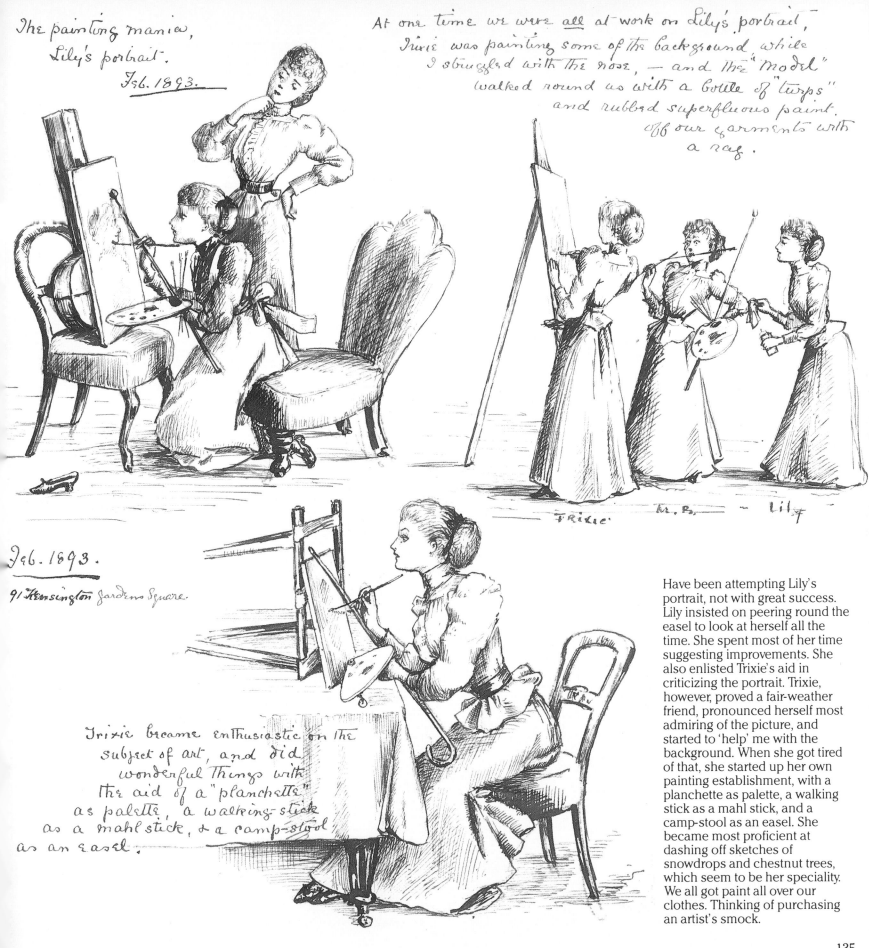

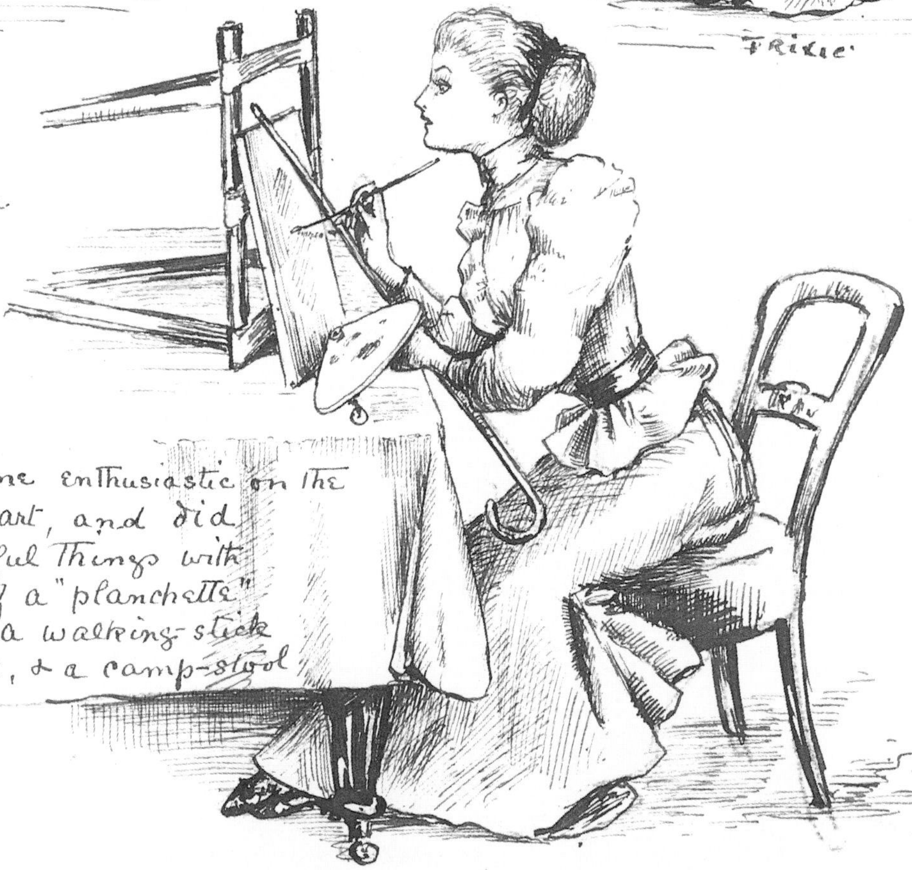

Trixie became enthusiastic on the subject of art, and did wonderful things with the aid of a "planchette" as palette, a walking-stick as a mahl stick, & a camp-stool as an easel.

Have been attempting Lily's portrait, not with great success. Lily insisted on peering round the easel to look at herself all the time. She spent most of her time suggesting improvements. She also enlisted Trixie's aid in criticizing the portrait. Trixie, however, proved a fair-weather friend, pronounced herself most admiring of the picture, and started to 'help' me with the background. When she got tired of that, she started up her own painting establishment, with a planchette as palette, a walking stick as a mahl stick, and a camp-stool as an easel. She became most proficient at dashing off sketches of snowdrops and chestnut trees, which seem to be her speciality. We all got paint all over our clothes. Thinking of purchasing an artist's smock.

April and July 1893

Easter Sunday

A dull day, we went to church morning and evening. Pat is in dire trouble. Ethel, being a most deedy cook, made some meringues for tea on Good Friday, which we much enjoyed. Two meringues only remained uneaten and Ethel put them aside for a rainy day. Unfortunately, she did not think to hide them from Pat. He discovered them today and ate them both before Ethel found out. Then, 'Vengeance is mine' said she, and beat him to bits with a scrubbing brush. The General told her it was only just that she be deprived of her sweetmeats, as only greed had led to her concealing them in the first place. A moral tale, which ends with Ethel in a sulk.

Made the sweetest little Easter jacket for Pat, to cheer him up. Cut some lambkins off the curtains in one of the attic rooms—which now look sadly ragged—sewed them onto a green felt jacket I ran up in a trice. When Pat ran round the room barking—he did not seem to like his festive rig at all—the lambs seemed to be gambolling at pasture. Just as I was about to take him for a walk, it struck me that I could give some religious significance to the coatee with very little trouble. I cut out yellow circles from Jim's straw hat and pasted them above my lambs' heads. Thus my lambs became Lambs of God with haloes. Rather a problem to know what to do with the remains of Jim's hat. In my enthusiasm I had forgotten it was his favourite headgear. Took it to the Park, in the end, for Pat to play with.

April 2nd 1893. Easter Sunday.
Ethel saved up two
meringues which Pat
discovered. He eat one, and
then returned for the other while
Ethel was beating him.

Awake all night, and on my knees at prayer for hours. The Easter coatee won much applause in the Park. Unfortunately, Colonel Clavering became quite blasphemous in his chaff, and booted poor Pat into the Round Pond. He wanted to see if he would walk on the water. Poor Pat was drenched, and the coatee a sodden rag. At home, Jim noticed his hat was missing. I said nothing, only detached a few shreds of straw from my guilty partner's collar. Helped Jim look in all the cupboards and under all the sofa cushions—of course, to no avail. Astonished by my powers of duplicity.

uly

Vent for a day out to Lord's 'ricket Ground. Beautiful day. 'he cricketers like white puppets ı an ordered dance on the green ward. Somerset was playing ssex. Watching the play made us ɔ thirsty, we retreated to the efreshment place to have that niversal panacea—a cup of tea. thel, here on a health visit from ıdia, behaved more oddly than sual, lost her umbrella down a rack between the boards and ıen spilt her cup of tea down her ress. The other ladies in efreshments did not know here to look. Ethel, as usual, lamed it all on her lassitudinous erves. Fortunately, on this ccasion she did not burst into ars—for which much thanks. ıe forgot her troubles when we ached home, and played appily with the cats till inner-time.

oing to Sandown for Lilian's edding to Fred. How long ago it eems when I first realized the epths of their feeling for one nother. It was when we went rimrose picking on Fred's rthday, and he presented Lilian ith the bunch he picked. Now ıey are to be married. My heart els very full. Jim has kindly ven me fifteen pounds with hich to buy a present. Bearing lian's sweet tooth in mind, ettled on a silver sugar dredger. eakie writes that, though she sapproves of the married state general, on this occasion she lents. She has promised the ir a set of silver salt cellars—to ld wit to their wedding.

ondered whether to take Pat th us, or leave him in London th Cook. The General assures e he would pine without us, and cast doubts on the staff's ability to look after him.

Judging by the dinners she served us, he said, there was no guarantee that Pat would not die of malnutrition while we were away. Very downcast by these aspersions on my Domestic Arrangements. Decided to take Pat with a good grace, though convinced he will only muddy our dresses, bark at all the children, and, in general, be a Dratted Nuisance.

It isn't safe to sit near Ethel at Lord's. July 1893.

Mr. F. Armstrong Boucher to Miss R. L. Black-Barnes.

On Monday last week (July 31) the wedding took place of Mr. Frederick Armstrong Boucher, son of Mr. J. B. Boucher, of Spring Villa, Sandown, Isle of Wight, and Rosalie Lilian Maud Mary, second daughter of Mr. William Black-Barnes, of Collingbourne Lodge, Sandown. The ceremony took place at half-past two in St. John's Church, Sandown, which had been beautifully decorated with flowers by personal frends of the bride. The bridegroom was accompanied by Mr. J. H. Sinclair as best man. The bride entered the church leaning on her father's arm. Her gown of ivory satin had a full Court train, and she wore a handsomely embroidered veil and orange blossoms. Of the three bridesmaids one was the bride's sister, Miss May Black-Barnes, and the other two the bridegroom's sisters, Miss Boucher and Miss Jessie Boucher. The first-named was in a becoming pink crépon, with pink satin sleeves and trimmings, and the latter looked equally well in pale green crépon and satin. Miss Evelyn Black-Barnes had on a tussore silk dress trimmed with pink silk and lace, and a hat to match. Among the friends present at the service and afterwards at the reception at Collingbourne Lodge were Mrs. Henry Pigeon, jun., Mr. and Mrs. Boucher, Mr. and Mrs. [illegible] Black-Barnes, General and Mrs. J. C. Berkeley, Miss Berkeley, Miss [illegible] Berkeley, Mrs. Malcolm Lyde, Canon Whitby, M.A., Miss Kathleen Fardell, Miss Parry, Mr. J. H. Sinclair, Mr. Herbert Whitby, &c. Mr. and Mrs. F. Armstrong Boucher left later in the afternoon for London, from whence they go on to various other places. The travelling dress worn by the bride was a grey tailor-made tweed, with large hat of burnt straw with feathers. The list of presents included :—

From Mr. F. A. Boucher, sapphire and diamond ring ; Miss Barnes, gold ring and diamond pin ; Mr. and Mrs. Boucher, dining-room clock and two bronze figures ; Mr. and Mrs. F. H. Boucher, fish knives and forks in case ; the Misses Boucher, worked skirt ; Mrs. Henry Pigeon, jun., silver coffee jug ; Miss J. Boucher, toast rack ; Mr. W. Boucher, Tantalus spirit stand ; Miss C. Boucher, tea service ; Mr. Black-Barnes, gold hunter watch ; Miss Mabel Black-Barnes, silver sugar basin and tongs ; Miss Evelyn Black-Barnes, pair of silver salt cellars in case ; Mr. Harold Barnes and Mrs. F. Black-Barnes, silver dessert knives and forks in case ; Mrs. F. Black-Barnes, afternoon teacloth ; Mr. F. Black-Barnes, R.N., case of large and small silver-mounted dinner knives ; Mr. Atherton, drawing-room clock ; General and Mrs. Berkeley, silver sugar dredger ; and many others.

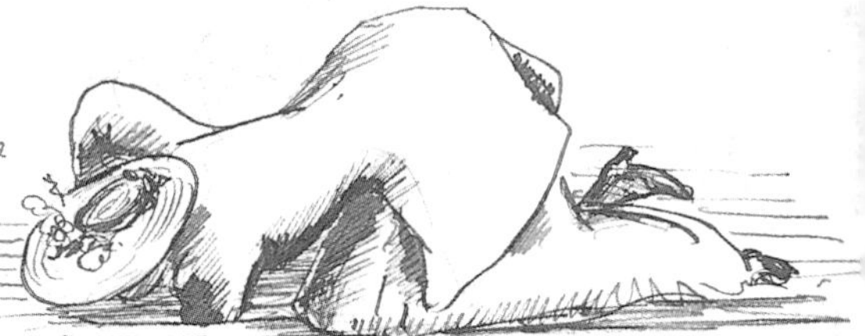

Ethel tried to see how far down her umbrella would reach—The result.

August 1893

"The Bath Bun" & his
Escort.
Sandown. ~~Sept.~~ 1893.
Aug.

Sandown
Aug. 1893.
"The Cat—

All my prognostications about Pat proved vain and empty. In Ruby Barnes and Edmund Meakins he has two devoted slaves. Ruby makes daisy chains by the mile to ring his collar, and there is no greater joy for Edmund than wrestling with Pat on the sands. 'Don't you bring 'm back all dishevelled again', Mrs Meakins warned me, and, oh dear, dishevelled again he went back. What is a little sand between friends? Or the ruination of a sailor suit?

Very nice to see the parents again. The Great G in an equable frame of mind, Nannie as tranquil as ever. They seem much older, however, to my dismay. The Great G's gout is still bad, despite Dr Blackie's remedies. Dr Blackie told me in confidence that, while the Great G continues to drink so much port, there is little chance of the gout ever diminishing. The Great G flew into a terrible rage when I mentioned this and told me not to listen to that fool doctor. Very upsetting. Wonder if I can get Nannie to substitute redcurrant cordial for the offending port. Wonder if Jim drinks too much. Raised the subject over dinner in the Pier Hotel, where we dined for a treat.

Jim's response was great amusement. Very upset. Even another bottle of champagne could not serve wholly to dispel my mortification.

We took poor Eddie Chambers out for an airing round Sandown. He lost a leg out on service in India in a gallant attempt to shoot a tiger. The tiger bit his leg off.

A stray kitten has adopted us. She has the sweetest habit of rubbing her back up against one's skirts. We call her Rubadubdub. She is not popular with all. Mrs Hatchet on a visit from the West Country, came to tea in a gown which defies description. Coquelicot and violet stripes on a cerise ground. On her orange curls, sat plumes and ribbons and rosettes of every hue. She looked just like a pantomime horse.

I complimented her on her gown. She was always used to dress like a Greek Woman in black drapes and sniff at our red frogged coats. All is explained. She lives next door to a lady artist who has persuaded her that she has an Astral Aura like Jacob's coat. It is imperative that she express this in her apparel. The only colour which clashes with her Aura, she informed us, is orange. At this point Rubadubdub rubbed up against The Enemy's skirts. To our horror, we observed that she left a fringe of fur behind her.

To divert attention, Jim lured poor Rubadubdub to the hosepipe and turned it on full. She yowled piteously. Jim informed me in a whisper that wet fur does not come off. As I went to rescue my poor puss, the hosepipe 'mysteriously' slithered over in my direction and sprayed me thoroughly. Mrs Hatchet sat throughout the palaver she had caused, complacent in her Aura. We were very glad when she left.

My husband tries the joke on me
but I don't see it!!

Astrophe"

September and October 1893

Mollie Boucher is now quite mistress of her home, though she has not married. Such a pity, such a cheerful girl. Her great height perhaps makes the men a little fearful. Jim calls her 'Juno'. She says she is resigned to being maiden aunt to all her relations' and friends' children. She has taken much of the burden of running Spring Villa from her mother's invalid shoulders.

Her great love is the greenhouse which Mr Boucher has added to the house. There she grows tobacco plants, chrysanthemums and miniature trees in great abundance.

Jim has just returned, hot and dusty from a walk into Ryde with Uncle Jossy. It seems they met Lady Daly in her finery outside a dressmaker's. Jim, though thinking her prinked out like a prize peacock, gave a civil good morning. She has become so grand since Sir James's ennoblement, she barely nodded a reply. And then she asked: 'Do tell, why is your friend wearing that handkerchief on his head. It looks so strikingly vulgar.' Jim was astonished by this rudeness and could only answer: 'Perhaps, then, you could lend him your parasol.' At which Lady Daly sniffed and flounced off to her waiting carriage. Jim says he and Uncle Jossy had to have a long drink of ale to get her out of their noses. And she never thought to ask after me.

Mollie has to lift up her friends when they wish to smell the flowers in her greenhouse.

J.C.B. walks into Ryde on a hot day with Uncle Jossy and meets Lady Daly.

October

Nice to be home, though we all enjoyed the summer at Sandown. All the girls have benefited, Trixie declares she does not know how I could bear to leave it. She would recite Lord Tennyson's lines 'Break, break, break, on thy cold grey stones, O sea', at breakfast, till we grew quite tired of the words and wished it had never came into his Lordship's mind to write them.

Jim is such an indulgent father to the girls. He worries so over their futures. I joke, that he need have no fears. They will all soon marry rich nabobs from India, live in pagodas and only travel on elephants with tusks sprinkled and studded with rubies. He tells me this is nonsense, but I distinctly saw Trixie atop an elephant in a dream. She was waving a parasol and looking very pretty.

Lily is as sweet as ever, always helpful about the house, and endlessly caring for all the waifs and strays of the area. Her hero is Lord Shaftesbury. She would love to emulate his example, and collect all the caged birds and pet dogs and kittens in Bayswater and set them free. She tells me also, by the bye, that she believes in the Brotherhood of Man.

Quite what this means, I am at a loss to discover. The only effect I have been privileged to suffer is that the new Girl is very upset. Lily went down to the kitchen and preached at her while she was making blancmange. The Girl could not follow a word of what Lily said, and interpreted the message to be that Jim should be doing the cooking. She laid down her tools, and, floury arms akimbo, came with Cook to my boudoir to complain of her wrongs. With the greatest possible difficulty, I persuaded her to return to her station.

Needless to say, the blancmange was lumpy and Jim complained. The cares of a busy household! To cap it all, Ethel saw a spider and had hysterics. Lily redeemed herself by quieting her with the aid of a dripping sponge.

Trixie is very quiet these days. I believe she is hopelessly in love with one of Jim's subalterns—young Conrad Phipps. Jim brought him here to dinner last week, and Trixie listened with rapt attention to his stories of the West Indies. She has never paid her father the compliment of listening to more than half one of his tales of the sub-continent. She also volunteered to play the piano after dinner, not a treat we are often offered. Sadly, Mr Phipps fell asleep while she was only half-way through the Second Movement. 'Music hath charms to soothe'. We all hoped that Mr Phipps might send round to invite Trixie out to tea. So far we wait in vain. She has taken to retiring into the next room after dinner and reading poetry, to our alarm.

Trixie finds our society too distracting when she wants to read — so retires into the next room.

Lily's cure for Ethel's hysterics
34 Lansdowne Crescent
Oct. 1893

"Aunt Prissy" thinks it must be raining.

December 1893

Ethel, Lily and I are taking a brave plunge today and going to Owen's to buy ourselves hats. Jim has been cajoled into giving us an untold number of guineas with which to purchase our finery. Trixie is in a puritan mood, and has elected to stay at home and read Temperance Tracts. I like the sober style in hats. As a General's wife, I feel I should command respect as well as present an attractive appearance. Lily and Ethel, with none of these considerations to bear in mind, have set their hearts on the most outrageously frilled and flowered pieces d'espièglerie.

Owen's proved a great success. We all found hats to suit our various whims. Madame de Lisle, the fitter, was most effusive in her praise of a monstrosity which she tried to force on Ethel. It dated from somewhere in the eighteenth century, we supposed, though Madame assured us it was in the latest mode.
She whispered that a certain lady, not unknown to the Prince of Wales, had thought very hard before deciding not to buy it. Well, we were not to be caught, either. I settled for a hat called *Fête Champêtre* of all unlikely names—an entrancing affair of straw and velvet ribbon.
Ethel decided on one with a few fetching plumes to dangle over one eye. And Lily bought a small hat with flowers to perch on her pretty blonde hair. We are all deeply grateful to Jim.

Trixie & The shoe horn!
Dec. 1893

Choosing hats at Owen's
Ethel. Now do you think this suits me?
Assistant. Oh Madam!! It is most becoming! I've never seen anyone look so beautiful in a hat

Most of today, we have written Christmas cards. There are so many to inscribe, I fear we shall never come to the end. We sent one to Frank and Downie, now blissfully married in New Brunswick. Lilian and Fred are still in Paris. Every letter I receive promises that they will return to England soon, and, with each letter, Lilian always encloses some French frippery. So how can I wish this delightful stream of presents to end? But I do think Fred should put his foot down, and end this ceaseless round of gaiety. For the parents, I have made a frivolous confection of tinsel and ribbon, which can go on the mantelpiece underneath the Great G's old canes.

Influenza has struck the household. We are all suffering from streaming colds and watery eyes and it is Christmas Day. Tim felt so poorly, he could barely see to carve the turkey. Lily has retired to bed with damp towels plastered to her forehead, and announced her decision not to rise again till the last flu-ridden germ has left her. Trixie plays mournful tunes on the piano all day. I seem set to celebrate Christmas alone with just the servants for company.

The cowl on the drawing-room chimney made a most blood-curdling sound.
30 Lansdowne Crescent.
Dec. 1893.

few of the
mas cards
ing to
post.

Dec. 1893.
Ethel during the late gale

January and February 1894

A very sad time. The Great G died peacefully at Sandown this month.

We have a new addition to the household—an adorable black kitten called Mr Joseph.
Lily found him in a back alley near here, prowling round the streets. She took him in, and, since then, he has had the household at his feet.
Jim declared, when I presented him with the *fait accompli* on his return home, that nothing would induce him to come to care for a cat. It was Jim who became dreadfully worried when bedtime came, and Mr Joseph had gone missing. He found him grubbing in the dirt outside.

We have bought Mr Joseph a new basket to replace the soft pile of cushions on which he has been sleeping. And Jim brought home the smartest of red collars to tie around his bonny neck, with a tag attached bearing the words—'Mr Joseph, 30 Lansdowne Crescent'.

Mr Joseph today attacked Trixie as she was reading in the drawing-room. He clawed at her wrist. Lily has now turned against her orphan babe, and says sadly, 'Once an alley cat, always an alley cat.' Poor Mr Joseph.

Mr Joseph has been more than usually naughty today.
We thought, as he had exiled himself from Lily's good graces, that we should train him to be a 'mouser'. Accordingly, we installed him in the kitchen,

Mr Joseph renders sleep impossible
Feb. 3rd

under Cook's watchful eye. No sooner were her eyes turned towards the stove, however, than Mr Joseph leapt into the batter mix standing on the kitchen table and got himself covered in yellow slime. And not a rat has been caught. We have taken him back into the folds of the drawing-room curtains where he sits, playing with the cords for hours.
A useless but pleasant ornament.

February

We all went for a solemn constitutional circumnavigating the Round Pond today, and Jim vowed that, before July, we would find a new home. Poor Jim, he suffers terribly through having no room he can properly call his own. 'Always picking my way through your painting and Lily's tapestry and Trixie's knitting', is Jim's view of our elegant life in the Lansdowne Crescent drawing-room. So a house with a smoking room must be found.

Had to prevent Lily from accosting two children dressed in ragged trousers and boots.
She was sure they were from an orphanage and needed mothering. I pointed out that they looked perfectly happy, shying stones at each other by the side of the pond. Why waste worry on them? As if to echo my words, there suddenly arose a monstrous shape in black bombazine and bonnet from a bench by the pond. She proceeded to cuff both boys then led them off like a zoo keeper, some troublesome whelps. If mother she was, then mother they had, as I pointed out to Lily.

March and April 1894

Blouse-making mania has broken out. Trixie began it when she boldly declared she was going to copy a model with long, puffed sleeves from *The Ladies' Pictorial*. Lily was so impressed by her sister's prowess, she followed suit. Jim did all he could to prevent me following my mad-cap step-daughters' example. But I would not be diverted from my purpose. I, too, cut and sewed and pinned till I near went distracted. Had to start again

We discover an original mann
of enjoying the unusually wa
weather.
March.

several times. Only the emergence of three perfect blouses brought the depredation on Derry and Tom's haberdasher department to a close.

Thought we would go for a spree to Kew Gardens today, as we are all feeling full of energy. Walked up to Notting Hill Gate, talking animatedly all the way about the different plants we wished to see. So busy were we chatting, we failed to spy the very omnibus we wanted speeding away down towards Shepherd's Bush.

Lovely walk round the Temperate House, a white iron cage for all sorts of pretty green plants. Particularly liked the plumbago. If we find a house with a conservatory, it could droop over the diners' heads very effectively. Did not like the Palm House so much. Though Lily and Trixie laughed at me for my fears, felt quite convinced some lions and tigers had accompanied the tropical plants from their native home. Several of the cacti looked quite ready to open ravening maws and swallow one entire.

pril

oday the dance at Addison all dawned. Trixie distinguished erself by getting lost for a good alf-hour with young Conrad hipps. There may be something ore there than meets the eye. m and I danced a stately minuet r two, but I am not really a great and at dancing. Those childish ears at Sandown when I danced night out four times a week eem aeons ago.

ly and Trixie went shopping day, down to Derry and Tom's nd back. Lily is in urgent need of some new petticoats. She tears hers to shreds quite casually. On the way, Trixie reported, Lily managed to hail an omnibus which was going in the wrong direction, halt it when she realized her error, and knock the driver's hat off when she finally managed to hail the right one. Trixie said her nerves were worn to a frazzle before they even entered Derry's. To compound her discomfort, Lily would ask for coloured zephyr and moirette petticoats. The shop assistant did not know what she was talking about. 'Here's the cotton, miss, them's the usual we sell here.'

April 1894.
HUDS

they Hurry up stairs

in search
of a cool
sitting-out place
and eventually
find themselves
back in the ball-room!!

and fly along corridors

May and June 1894

We are having a very difficult time with Mr Joseph. Sometimes it seems as though he does not wish to live with us at all.

June

We are footsore and weary, having tramped the streets of North Kensington from morning to midnight. Jim refuses to live south of the Park, a decision no doubt influenced by the fact that both Sir George Berkeley and Lady Peile live north of it.
My wishes were not consulted in the matter, though I have a preference for leafy Chelsea. Every day, from noon to dusk, we walk out with a spring in our step, accompanied by Mr Snigg, the estate agent. Every evening we return, having been over a number of residences—none of which fit the bill. Jim turned against one otherwise pleasant house, for the sole reason that a foul smell of cabbage pervaded the kitchen quarters. Lily objected to another on the grounds that there was a very rowdy public house on the corner. 'What if some drunken comrades came out and assaulted me?' was her complaint. Trixie took strongly against a third on the grounds that she would have to sleep in the garret.

Mr Snigg was despairing. The top hat he clutched nervously as he extolled the charms of each residence became more and more battered. One dark June day, as the rain pelted outside, we

stood round a room with an ugly fireplace, which put it quite out of the question. Mr Snigg clutched his battered hat and said, 'Then there is Linden Gardens.' Almost before he spoke, I knew that Linden Gardens would answer.

It is perfect. Close to Kensington Gardens, just behind the shops in Notting Hill Gate, it is a little jewel of a house with six bedrooms, two reception rooms and a smoking room, plus ample kitchen quarters for the staff. The girls chose their bedrooms happily, quite oblivious of the fact that an old grandmother was asleep in bed in one of the rooms, and two tiny tots crying in the other. The General and I found our quarters — bedroom, boudoir and dressing-room — very acceptable.

Thirty feet of the greenest grass stretch out from french windows to a gnarled cherry tree at the foot of the garden. Jim and I are equally enthusiastic about this. He plans to grow the Bourbon roses he loves; I plan to pick his roses to adorn delicate tea-parties on the lawn.

A highly desirable residence in an eminently quiet and fashionable position!

July 1894

What long and weary hours have we spent, choosing furniture and decorations for the house. For the drawing-room, we chose a magnificent blue carpet decked with roses. Jim wanted a sober beige, as Anna Sophia had had. The girls and I prevailed. Whiteleys had just the thing we desired for curtains—a bale of Chinese patterned silk.
My extravagance made poor Jim blench, but I believe quality speaks for itself. We also chose linen antimacassars and tablecloths and napkins from a rich store of such delights.
For chairs and tables and beds, we made our way to Christie's salesroom, and bid feverishly for set after set of dining-room chairs. In some we were successful; others went for too high a price. Our meals became meetings of Council, where we debated the virtues of mahogany against teak, planned attacks on furniture warehouses and worried, worried, worried. Friends came with advice, some good, some bad. In one ear it went and out the other as we pursued errant sideboards, glasses and jugs. As we had not unpacked all of our wedding presents, we found to our delight that we had several decanters and more than enough china with which to start our new life.

In the midst of all this flurry and bustle, I suddenly contracted the most dreadful toothache. At first I kept it quiet, not wishing to be distracted from the main task, and—dare I confess—reluctant to face the pain of the dentist's chair? Night after night I lay silent with my pain. Dear Jim noticed nothing. It was only when my jaw began to swell that the girls and Jim realized there was something amiss. To protests that I was fine, really, Trixie inexorably led me to the dentist's. With fear and trepidation, I awaited my fate. Mr Simpkins, the dentist, came out, smiled falsely, and beckoned me to his chair. He prepared to administer laughing gas. At which point Trixie fainted and had to be led from the room.
Then Mr Simpkins's drill descended and I knew no more.

We quit Lansdowne Crescent today, after months of preparation. Feel quite sorry to be leaving, though excited about the new house. More trunks and packing cases have rarely been seen. Besides all the clothes we have accumulated, there is my library of novels, Jim's military regalia, and Lily's canary to transport. And Mr Joseph, of course. The driver of the wagon we hired could not be persuaded to take all of us at once. So Jim and the girls went on ahead, and I followed on foot with the Girl and

We spent many long & weary hours during July choosing furniture, decoratio

ɪr Joseph. A pleasant walk ırough the squares and busy treets of North Kensington. 'assed friendly Mrs Martin at her ruit stall in Portobello Lane. She ave me a ruddy-cheeked apple or luck when I told her we were noving house.

Departure from 30 Lansdowne Crescent July 29th 1894

oceeded a little further and in otting Hill Gate, we met Conrad ipps. Have not heard from him a long time. Impetuously ked him to come and be the st visitor to grace our happy me. He obliged, and, to our light, bought from a vintner's a ttle of champagne. Our toasts the new house did rather convenience Jim and the bbie as they tried to dispense e furniture and trunks about the use. Both Jim and the cabbie eered up considerably, I am d to say, over a glass of ampagne. A lovely first night in r first real home.

August and September 1894

A few of the girls following Uncle Jossy out of the ice-shop.
Sandown - August. 1894.

That garden hose gave us many an unexpected & pleasant surprise.

ery reluctant to leave Linden
ardens so soon after our
istallation. Promised Nannie,
owever, that we would come to
andown. Although she has
mmie living with her now, she
rites that she still misses the
reat G daily. Such a long and
appy marriage. Pray that Jim and
can be as content. Wanted to
ay with Nannie, but, as all the
ils have come too, Jim has
ken a house looking on to the
ea front.

ook Nannie for a walk in her
ath-chair along the esplanade.
he seemed to recover some of
er former vigour, and begged
m not to push the chair quite so
st. She had no time to greet
cquaintances, she said grandly.
elieve she will become the
owager Empress of Sandown in
time, receiving tributes from
er people.

ent with the girls to Beti's tea
op for old times' sake.
hough it was perfectly agreeable, memories of the old days when Harold Pope occasionally treated me to an ice flooded back. Lilian, I am sure, would never think such a thing. Could not help looking round the tea shop for old friends seated in corners. To my great surprise, Mollie Boucher came in just as I had searched the room and discovered all were strangers. Going to visit and admire the garden she has made at Spring Villa tomorrow. She tells me, to my horror, that she is now so wedded to the single state, she means to set up house in Ventnor with a friend and live out the rest of her days on the Island. I know Mollie was never an ambitious girl. Could not but think it sad, none the less.

Nannie has let the garden at Fernside go to rack and ruin. All the flower beds are overgrown with weeds, and, from the ornamental urn in the centre of the lawn, sprouts a wild crop of dandelions. Jim and the girls and I volunteered to weed it all out. Then Nannie can sit outside in her basket chair and enjoy these summer afternoons.

We dug and weeded and planted till all the garden was returned to its former glory. Out came the bracken and fern and dry sticks, and in went chrysanthemums and Michaelmas daisies, snapdragons and stocks. We planted a Virginia creeper very neatly so it would twine its red-gold way up the wall of the house. Jim dug the dandelions out of the urn, and filled it with water for the sparrows to drink. We put ivy and geraniums in delightful little hanging baskets. Then the real fun began, when we started to water all the plants. The hose would sprinkle unwary observers from a hole half way down the tube. Poor Jim had the misfortune to be caught twice.

September

Nobody else came forward. The younger generation are very slack. So we were the sole performers at the Brading Primrose League Entertainment. Much enjoyed ourselves, and dear Major Brown said afterwards he had not enjoyed such music since I married and left the Island. He has an odd idea of enjoyment. His snores punctuated our strummings on the banjo. I accepted the compliment in the friendly spirit in which it was made.

We were the sole performers at
the Brading Primrose L. Entertainment.
Sep. 1894. Sandown.

October to December 1894

Journeyed back to London safely, except for one incident at Sandown station, when Lily and Mr Joseph seemed like to be attacked by rabid dogs.
Very pleased to be settling into Linden Gardens at last.
Had dreadful dreams, between Portsmouth and London, of the house engulfed in flames. Relieved to see it still standing.

Lily and I went shopping.
The small legacy I had from the Great G has been enormously helpful, now that we are furnishing our house. Sneaked out today with Lily, because I wanted to buy Jim a mirror and a footstool for his smoking-room. He would certainly refuse to allow me to 'waste my blunt', as he calls it, on him, so I had to take great care to deceive him as to the purpose of our jaunt. Said we were off to a dancing class.

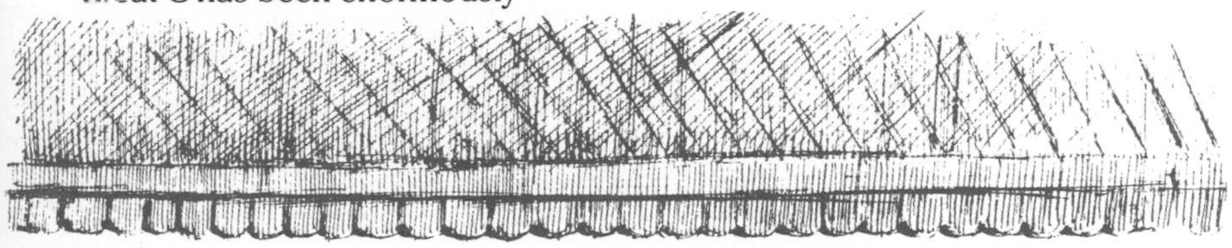

"Auntie" in charge of little "Josy"
at the Sandown station
Mi-aw—Mi-aio!
Oct. 1st 1894.

Found just the mirror to suit Jim' plain tastes—golden pilasters at each side and a wreath over the top. Dare not put down how much it cost. The footstool is as important. Although dear Jim is sober man I fear that his occasional consumption of port may well lead to gout. Did not mention this to Lily, as I did not wish needlessly to alarm her. Nevertheless, insisted we found one and would not return home till we had the prize. Just as our tempers were fraying nicely, found the exact stool of my dreams. Walnut, with a tapestrie and beaded top.

Jim was delighted with both the presents. Spurred on to greater things, he hung the mirror. Then before resting his leg on th footstool, he hung the cupboard in the dining room—a troublesome task which he has been putting off since we bough it. I arranged all our glasses on the shelves, and we sat down to very good dinner. It was a new dish I had had Cook make—co with a prawn sauce.

Putting up the dining-room cupboard.

Oct. 1894 4 Linden Gardens.

Picture hanging Nov. 1894 4 Linden Gardens

November

Besides finding out where all the best provisions in the area are to be had here, not done a great deal this month. The girls and I spend our days very happily, sewing a little, marketing in Portobello Lane, and thinking where to put new items as we buy them. When Jim is at home, as he frequently is, thank heavens, we commit our puny strength to tasks of greater moment.
Last weekend, for example, we hung all the pictures. Now Jim's father and mother frown at our frivolous meals, and a charming Rosetti 'Belle Dame sans Merci' gazes down at our bed.

what led him to leave us. Hung a notice on the railings: 'Lost. Black cat answering to name, Mr Joseph. Reward to finder.' So far, no one has called except one old gentleman in a frock coat who said a black cat had savaged his ginger. Not our Mr Joseph who has the most distinguished manners.

Happy day. Jim has had the splendid notion of purchasing another cat. He brought home in his overcoat pocket the most delightful soft, squirming bundle of velvety fur. We have named her Jodie, and propose to love her as fervently as we did Mr Joseph. She has one peculiarity which would be useful, were she to get lost. She squawks rather than mews. Last night we had a fine example of this. While listening to Jim's rhythmical breathing, I was suddenly aware of plaintive intermittent squawks emanating from down below. Tiptoed out in my night-gown to find that Lily

"Jodie" came to prayers and sat on my back.
Sunday. Jan. 13th 1895.

A consultation as
to whether "Jodie"
is to be brought up
from the kitchen
to spend the night
with Lily.
— if "Jodie" squawks
once more that is
to decide the
question.

Listening for "Jodie's" squawk. Jan. 8th 11. p.m

and Trixie had also been woken. The squawks became more plaintive. I reproached myself for having left poor Jodie down in the kitchen without any company. On the other hand, Jim would reproach me if I brought the little cat to sleep in our room.

"Impudence and Dignity"
I.C.B. and Léon Pont.

The whole family rush to wait on "Jodie" when she squawks.

Lily, thank heavens, came to the rescue and, from now on, Jodie is to sleep in her room. At prayers this morning, however, it was my back on which she elected to settle.

Had a visit from Jim's little godchild, young Léon Pont. His English grandmother, Countess Marchand, brought him to tea. In her august presence, none of us dared converse except in the most strained and polite voices. She is very high in the instep and smiled only at little Léon's childish blunders. When I offered him a drop-scone, being unused to English teas, he took it and dropped it on the floor with an angelic smile. 'Drop scone', he repeated. How we did laugh. Jim adores Léon, and loves being a godfather. After tea, he talked man to man to Léon in the smoking room, while we entertained the Countess. She unbent a little and described every ailment from which she had suffered in the past year. It was a fascinating list. Jim exchanged hats with Léon for a joke, tipped him a half a sovereign, and then the visit was at at end.

"Countess M....." to Trixie: Seeing you again is quite like old times.
(Trixie never having seen her before)

February and March 1895

Irixie's going to skate

Irixie returning from the Round Pond
(The one-legged sweeper to the rescue)

1st day's skating. Feb. 1st 1898.

J.C.B.

The obstreperous patient who insisted on having a bath while his temperature was 102.5°.

The Influenza set in, Feb. 19th

The greatest victim – J.C.B. – was sent to bed; the others were dealt with collectively

Wednesday. Feb. 20th 1895.

What a February this has been. Nothing but slippery snow and over you go. And now the influenza has set in and threatens all the household. Too exhausted to write further.

The storms and rages in my head have abated somewhat. Poor Jim has got the influenza very badly. Now I am a second growth invalid, I spend my days dousing his forehead with damp cloths, and forcing him to drink my excellent lemonade when he calls for whisky.

Today, Jim insisted on having a bath, despite Dr Plunket's advice and a temperature of over 102°F. We were all very worried but it made him much more amenable, later in the day. Persuaded him to eat some thin gruel at four this afternoon.

Going to Owen's Sale - directly after breakfast.
M.B. & Lily
March - 1895.
Where can that pattern have gone

M.B. Now why should my skirt hang like that!
L.B. Could you possibly have put the side breadth in the front?
March 1895. Dressmaking continues through the month.

Returning from Owen's Sale at 1.30.
Crushed by the Crowd.

March

Lovely weather. Lily and I decided to take advantage of a free day to go and pick up bargains at Owen's sale. Pored over damask napkins. Lily longed for new gloves. Returned battered and bruised without either, but with several useless items in the way of brass pepper-mills, lip salve, and a dozen lavender soaps. Never again. The brass pepper-mills don't even grind.

4 Linden Gdns.

Spent the afternoon much more agreeably, choosing patterns for summer blouses and skirts.
I mean to make two voile blouses and a linen skirt. Lily is thinking of investing in a tennis outfit for Sandown. She is keen as mustard after last year's successes.
She twice won most covetable prizes—a gold mesh purse, and an emerald paste brooch.

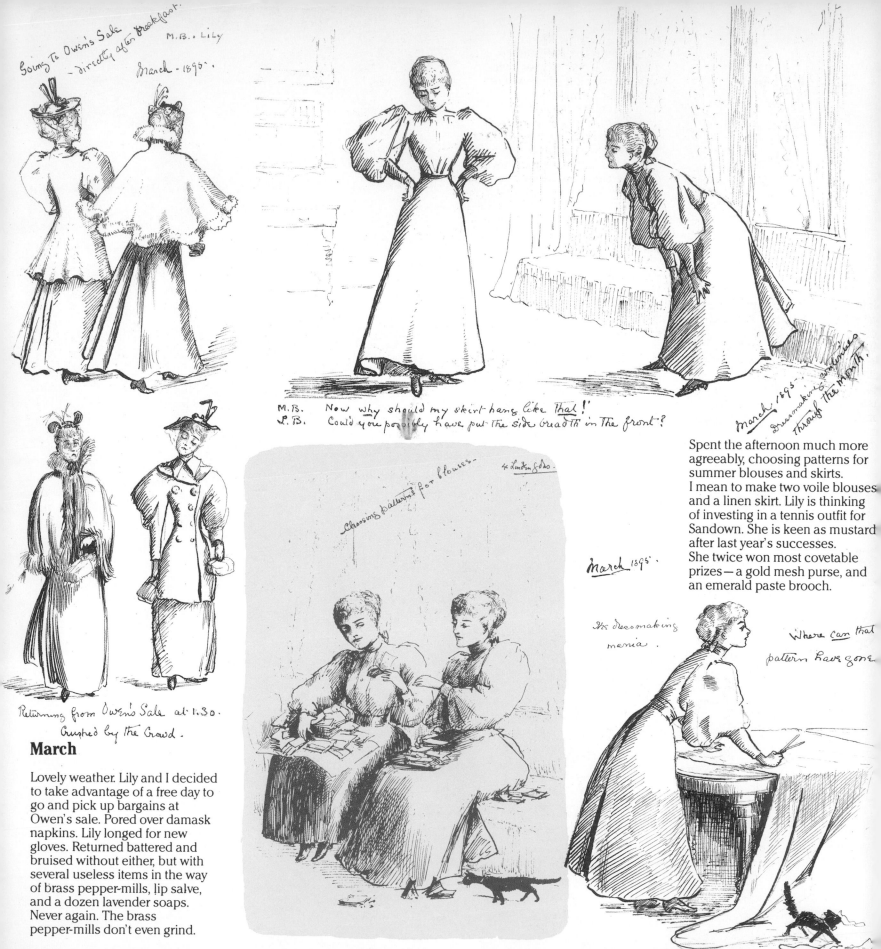

May to July 1895

ir George, Jim's brother, proposed that Lily and I should ome over to Hyde Park Iansions while Jim is so busy. Never loth to visit dear Jim's elations, but Hyde Park Iansions a little austere for my aste. Sir George has no feeling or those homely touches which can bring a room to life. I recommended, for instance, throwing a length of grey velvet, with peacock's feathers worked in, over the drawing-room door — as much to exclude the dreadful draughts in the flat as to provide an ingenious decoration. Sir George was, for a moment, roused to a pitch of enthusiasm one does not normally expect from him. Then he relapsed into his usual quietude, and muttered that it would not answer. The girls pressed him, but he said he was quite satisfied with the degree of decoration he had achieved on retiring from the West Indies. He saw no point in altering anything. Oh, Messrs Morris and Burne-Jones, no customer for you here.

Took our musical instruments at great cost to life and limb across the crowded streets of London. North Kensington and Paddington looking very bonny in the sunlight, we thought. I expressed my private conviction that the white stucco of the houses north of the Park excel all others for reasons of aestheticism and

We took our musical instruments to 10 Hyde Park Mansions May 1st
Lily kept on exhorting me to hold up my case like she did hers. or I should trip over it-!!

"Follow the Guv'ner! The Guv'ner's doing very well."

convenience. Lily was not listening, being overcome with desire to help some poor kitten which had unaccountably wandered out onto the crossing. She dropped her guitar case, scooped up the poor animal and deposited it in the arms of the crossing sweeper. He looked quite amazed by this presumption, as he had been quietly leaning on his brush, watching the world go by. A silver coin and an injunction to buy the poor mite some milk and a herring made him no less perplexed by the philanthropist lady, but he went off to do Lily's bidding.

Lady Peile, I think, enjoyed the musical entertainment we gave her after tea, though, at one point when I looked up from my old banjo, her eyes appeared to be closed, as though in restful slumber. When we had done, she contributed some weak applause and suggested she play us some Bach. Dear Lady Peile became quite lost in her music. I had no idea how long the somewhat laboured performance might last, and I was in an agony to get home. Cook, I knew, was preparing Jim's specially requested favourite pudding. At last, with a rattle of pearls, the performance came to an end and we made good our escape.

Dear Jim suggested today that we make an excursion to Hampton Court. Accordingly, we donned our best hats, left instructions for Cook to prepare against our return in the evening, and sallied forth in search of a hansom cab. Spied a very fine fellow, with a grey top hat and a dahlia in his buttonhole, cracking his whip in Notting Hill Gate. We all embarked with a good deal of cheeriness, and then floated through the streets of London with the greatest of ease till we reached the tram. It took us, with a great many stops and waits for changes of passengers, to Hampton Court. It was a glorious day—we had a picnic under a spreading vine—made even more so by Mrs Hatchet's benevolence in sending us some real Devonshire cream. She has moved to the West Country, to the delight of all in Sandown.
The General drank ale, while the girls and I stuck manfully to lemonade.

We contrived to lose ourselves entirely and without hope of redemption in the Maze, then returned home full of the highest spirits and prepared to discuss the iniquities of Cardinal Wolsey at length after our lectures from the guide.

Icy weather. Muffled myself up in a selection of Anna Sophia's shawls from Kashmir. Lily and Trixie have both assured me they feel no sense of chagrin at seeing the wraps of their beloved mama about my unworthy shoulders.

Wonder whether to bring out the garnet and oak set once more. Lily turned tearful when I first wore it. Trixie choked, and Ethel looked fixedly at my festooned ears and throat before going quickly from the room. Have since discovered these trinkets were only worn by dear Anna Sophia to servants' balls. What she wore on grander occasions, there is no telling. Certainly nothing survives except some tawdry seed-pearls.

Jim came home early. We had a very cheery tea with Sally Lunn cakes and jam by the fire, while the rain spluttered outside.

Eaton Mascott Hall
May 30th
View from the side of house

In spite of all the good advice so freely given we invariably hit the ball on the wrong side if we don't miss it altogether
Eaton Mascott Hall
Shrewsbury
May 24th to June 8.

June

Jim's old friends from India, the Jacksons, have invited us all to stay at their home, Eaton Mascott, in Worcestershire. Delighted to be going into the country on such a pleasant venture. A trifle nervous as to their reception of me. They were great friends of Anna Sophia's, so Lily and Trixie tell me. Know I can never replace her in many people's hearts. Hope for the best. Jim is such a support.

Such a lovely house. General Jackson a poppet and Mrs Jackson very kind. We have the finest of bedrooms, with a sofa piled with lace cushions, and a fine southerly view of the Malvern Hills. Feel we shall be very happy here.

Uncle Jossy, Jim's brother, is here, always sure to make a blunder or two. He insisted on playing billiards last night, when he had drunk too much champagne. He leant across the table with his cue, slipped and tore the baize cover from head to foot. There was a hushed silence, and then the General said very quietly 'Kindly leave.'

We were all most upset; poor Uncle Jossy can't help being clumsy. Being a naval man, he copes well with the swell of the ocean, but is unhinged by dry land. Thank heavens, the General relented and Uncle Jossy did not suffer the ignominy of being packed off on the milk train. Nevertheless, the billiard room door remained firmly closed for the duration of his visit.

Lovely day today. Organized a children's picnic for the Jackson brood and their Nicholson cousins, while their parents were away at a wedding. Martha, the Jacksons' capable cook, made us sausage rolls and egg and cress sandwiches and meringues, and packed them up very neatly in a hamper. Jim carried the rugs, Lily and Trixie and I, baskets of fruit and nuts, Uncle Jossy the wine and lemonade. We picnicked in a wood not far from the house. Never seen Jim so relaxed.

He told the children stories, and juggled apples in the air, and started a game of hide-and-seek. Young Charlie Nicholson took the game rather too much in earnest. He hid so well in the crook of an old beech tree, that no one could find him and we began to worry that he was lost. Thankfully, Charlie got bored and hooted like an owl, so we found him.

Note the typical ramshackle way in which we left our country paradise.

We left Eaton Mascott Hall

The Children's picnic in the wood
Eaton Mascott Hall. 28th June 1896.

July

Had a lovely day out at Lord's, watching the Varsity match. Lily and Trixie are indefatigable supporters of Oxford. I have a penchant for Cambridge, brother Herbert having attended there. We all cheered loudly, anyway, whenever anyone hit a ball for six. The finer points escape us, though Trixie declared roundly that she could do better than some of the young men on the field. This almost led her to blows with a forbidding matron carrying a pink parasol. 'One of the young men you refer to is my son, madam', she hissed. We moved away swiftly.

Had a dreadful, disaster-ridden dinner when we invited Conrad Phipps to dinner. A moth got into the smoking room, and the whole family turned coward and flinched from the attack. Only Jim and Mr Phipps were brave enough to go after it. Wished Trixie had not shown herself in quite such an unmartial light, quivering behind the armchair. No way to impress a military man. He needs steel in a wife. Mr Phipps thanked me very warmly for a most entertaining evening, but fear he will not readily return.

August to October 1895

Our new toy
Sept. 27th
4 Linden Gdns.
The family assembles in the hall 5 minutes before the clock strikes

My new passion is bicycling. Sandown is a different place, when transformed by the iron machine. I fly about the town with the greatest of ease, greeting friends with a nonchalant wave of the hand. Steakie is an old hand at the game. She has been riding a bicycle now for several years. She consents very kindly to join me on my wavering way to the Island's beauty spots. To think I wasted all my youth on trains and

My first attempt at bicycling.
Aug. 1895. Sandown
I tried to go stra
on but the bicycl
insisted on careerin
round an austere fem
who expressed strong
disapproval in every featur

n cabs when there was this ılternative. Have persuaded Trixie o take up the sport, so we can fly ıbout Kensington when we eturn home. Jim advises caution. Ie fears for our lives when we go ɔut on our jaunts. Tried to ɔersuade him to accompany us, ɔut he will not be caught. 'No use eaching an old dog new tricks', ıe says, so we have to be ;atisfied with describing to him ›very step of our journey.

›eptember

im went off to his tailor's this norning, saying mysteriously that ve should expect a surprise later. ıt twelve o'clock, the door ːnocker beat a tattoo. Standing ›n the step was a gentleman with ›range hair, and a gigantic crate ›eside him. On inviting him to ›tate his business, he spoke: 'I'm lelivering your grandfather.')reams of avatars brought to life vere dispelled when he ːxplained further: 'Yer husband ›ought it yesterday.' Jim has ›ought a grandfather clock. It is ›ur new toy. We assemble in the ıall five minutes before it strikes ınd Jim does wonderful things vith the pendulum and weights ı its inside. It is the greatest ›ossible success.

I am coming round, now that
my temperature is 'oval".

October

Went to visit Mabel, the parlour maid, who was rushed to the Middlesex Hospital last week. Jim awoke in the middle of the night to hear blood-curdling groans from up above. He took a candle and went to investigate. Poor Mabel was lying on the floor of her attic bedroom, clutching her side in despair. Her face was flushed and hot with tears. Fortunately, Jim was able to summon Dr Plunket from his home in Hereford Mansions close by, else who knows what might have occurred? Mabel seemed close to death! Dr Plunket diagnosed rheumatic fever, and whisked her into hospital. All is now in his capable hands. Meanwhile, we do very deedily for ourselves all Mabel's little tasks. We dust and polish and bring in the tea with such alacrity that Jim jokes he will turn Mabel away. When he has three such willing maids, what need of more, he reasons.

I have a peculiar method of dismounting
which Lily finds a little disconcerting.
Pride goes before a fall.

The Girls Fly the Nest

1896

January to March 1896

Dreadful news. Shame for England. A Dr Jameson has led a Revolution against President Kruger in the Transvaal. The Boers have surrounded Jameson and his men. *The Times*, Mr Rhodes and Mr Chamberlain are all implicated in the Raid. No one talks of anything else all over England. Jim buys each new edition of the paper as it comes out. I have temporarily forsworn the theatre of war, and am busy sorting out last year's receipted bills.

A new occupation. Went to stay last year with Jim's Aunt Lulu in Wales. Much admired her style of good, plain cooking. I was too loud in my praise. She has sent me a bundle of cookery books, with suitable recipes ringed in green ink. And she means to visit us in March to sample the results.

Lily and I have formed the habit of walking each day up to the Marble Arch, browsing in the shop windows of Notting Hill Gate as we go, and then enjoying the pleasant green breezes which waft across the railings of the Park. Each day, we pass a poor creature with a flat cap and an old tweed coat. He lolls by the side of the road with a few crude pictures chalked on the pavement beside him. Each day, we give him a few coppers, and each day we vow to pass by on the other side of the road. Jim would probably disapprove if he knew how we throw good money after bad.

February

Decided to do a little renovation and refurbishing about the house. In this cold weather, one does not feel like venturing out. Lily found an old book in the attic called *A Hundred and One Household Hints*. It has proved very useful. With its aid, we have got stains off shirts, removed wax drips from candlesticks and done any amount of other useful little tasks. At present we are making lampshades. Lily insisted we both make one. As we only have one lampstand big enough for the monsters we are making, we will have to go to the expense of buying another lampstand. But such is life!

March

This month we have progressed to making curtains for our bedroom. Since we settled here, we have made do with a peculiar blanket arrangement over the window. Jim pandered to my wish to find the curtains of my dreams. I found the exact shade of primrose silk I wanted for the drawing-room almost immediately. Whiteley's had bales of it. Try as I might, however, I could not find the Arthurian curtains I wanted for the bedroom — white with red fleur-de-lys boldly patterned to match the Queen Guinevere bed. (Jim laughs at my fancies, but our carved and painted bedhead is just like that of Queen Guinevere in my children's book of Arthurian legends.)

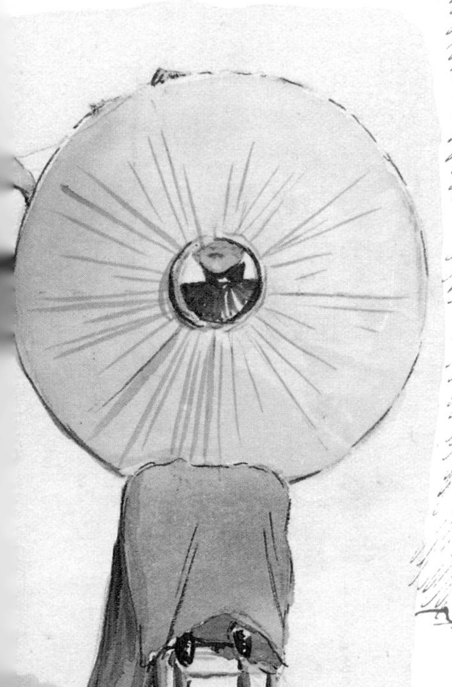

Trixie helping me to
take the dreadful curtain
that would not go right.
March 9th 1896.

Coming back from "Alfred Days" in The Bus.
"To seat 6 persons each side"

We had a carriage stuffed with moths on our way to Shrewsbury.

The very day Jim said he had complained for the last time about the blanket, and we must have proper curtains. I wandered down Portobello Lane, distractedly wondering where in heaven's name to find curtain material. Any curtains would do. I wanted them to be hanging on Jim's return.

All of a sudden, a little old Chinese gentleman with a black satin hat on his head popped out of a shop crowded with serendipity. 'Missee come', he beckoned and full of curiosity I entered. I felt like Aladdin of the pantomime, with he the genie who appeared when I rubbed the lamp. Not knowing what to expect, I looked round the crammed shop hesitantly, walked about, touched a brass lamp just for luck ... and then I saw it. Draped over a screen in the furthest corner of the room, across a nigh impenetrable forest of chair legs, was a sheet of brocade. Fleur-de-lys on a blue ground, as I live.

'You like?' the little Chinaman said, seeing my excitement. I nodded vigorously, praying there was enough material for curtains. He dragged the sheet out, and there was providentially more than three yards' length in it. Blessing my saviour for my release from misery, I paid my little Chinaman and rushed home with the material before it and the shop could vanish into thin air. Now all we have to do is make the wretched things.

We find ...
that the difficulties of
modern
life
what with flies ...
and moths
are sometimes past all
endurance.

August 1896

We spent a very agreeable month at Eaton Mascott with the Jacksons. One of the main divertimenti was a telescope, very like the one the boys of St Peter's presented to the Great G on his retirement. General Jackson is a keen astronomer, so I was privileged on several evenings to stand with him on the terrace under the stars, and trace, with him, their passage across the sky. The General jokes that he has no conservatory, only an Observatory

"Taking The sun"
at Eaton Mascott

going to bed with our
little tapers at Eaton
Mascott Hall
Aug. 1896

Jim and I have had several long walks in the park. Roaming cattle always near at hand, but they seem relatively friendly. Among other things, we have talked of the girls' future. Jim worries that, though they know many young men, nothing ever comes of it. Distressed, but had to admit it. Jim talks darkly of desperate measures. Not sure what he means. Went on a very jolly outing to Preen Manor to visit the Ashcombes. On the way, a drove of pigs got in front of us and we had great difficulty in turning them back.

Several very wet days. We told stories, and roasted chestnuts by the fire. The billiard room was much frequented. Agnes, Mrs Jackson, gave us a very good tip. If venturing out after a rainstorm, wear snow boots to save damage to shoe-leather. She led the way by going in her boots to cut roses for the dinner-table after the most torrential downpour. So fascinated by her example, got up at six o'clock to go 'egging' with her—

Aug 14th 1896

in snow boots. Able to tell Jim proudly at breakfast that I had personally found the speckled brown egg he was eating. He said he was very grateful for the information.

Went over to Ashtead to visit Agnes's sister and family. Found two artists hard at work on pictures for their mother's birthday. Could not forbear to paint them as they toiled.

November and December 1896

he desperate measures of which
n spoke, with regard to the
rls' future, have come to
uition — Jim is resolved to send
em to India, to seek their
rtunes and husbands there.
e has had word that Jim
ongridge, a subaltern in his
giment, has become something
a nabob. Jim tells me that
oung Jim always hankered after
y. She refused to countenance
s advances, saying that she had
her fish to fry than impecunious
ficers. Since she has heard of
s rise in the world, a portrait of
n has mysteriously surfaced to
r dressing-table. If I mistake
t, also, a letter addressed to
y came with an Indian stamp
st week. I am to tax Lily, on
n's instructions, with this
idence of an understanding,
morrow. What will come of it,
aven knows. Feel rather hurt
at Lily has allowed me to
ance up the garden path,
viting young men to the house
r her delectation. Wonder if
xie, too, has deceived us all
ese years.

y is in heaven. The letter that
me from India was from Jim.
wrote that he could not declare
love earlier. A Kashmiri rajah's
our has led to untold wealth.
proposes she come out to
lia immediately to join him.
, secretive soul that she is, has
gged her secret to herself all
se days.

at sadness and what joy.
all so miss our daily walk to the
rble Arch, and all the little

jokes we share. Lily's happiness must come first, however, and now her place is with her Jim, as mine is with mine. Trixie is to travel out in time for the wedding, and act as bridesmaid. We live in hope that she will form an alliance out there.
So we have two trousseaux to make before Lily, and then Trixie, set off. The house has been turned upside down, and we have made a variety of trips to tropical outfitters. Lily and Trixie are now the proud owners of two pith helmets. Jim swears they are invaluable in the jungle.
Trixie took fright at this. It was over tea, and she spilt her cup on the new carpet. Such accidents will never provide her with a helpmeet. She declared she was not going to India to live in the jungle. She plans to go to Poona, which we hear is the most civilized part of India. And her father's name will stand her in good stead.

The trunks are packed.
A hundred little things to do at th
last minute are done. Cousin
Harriet came round with farewell
presents from the girls' uncle and
aunt—and stayed to add her
weight to the trunk lid which
would not shut. Suddenly felt ver
miserable. How much I depend
on Lily. Had a mad impulse to
throw up Linden Gardens and
embark with them on a new life,
new adventure. These thoughts
swiftly passed from my mind, bu
as we all felt a mite anxious, we
had a rousing game of Animal
Grab to chase away the clouds.

Dreadful bad luck has befallen
us. Jim is very ill, with a
temperature of 104°F, so our pla
to go together and see Lily off on
HMS *Himalaya* has fallen by the
wayside. Lily is very upset, leavin
her father in his poorly state. I fe
anxious about every one. Today i
an ash-heap day, such as I have
not had since a girl.

he doctor has come, and Uncle ossy has turned up trumps and worn to escort Lily all the way to he *Himalaya*. Feel curiously onely without her. Jim is in a everish state and not minded for dle chatter, in any case. Vonder if the two of us will not ather rattle around in this big ouse when Trixie follows on. ime will tell, and time may bring velcome additions to the family.

ecember

ovely letter from Lily, headed: he Chapel of Bones, Malta. he is greatly enjoying the boat life. Lily writes that she has played deck quoits every afternoon with a spry young officer called Jim Nelson. Hope she does not mean to forget Jim Longridge before she reaches India. Trixie has done a lot of needlework in preparation for her departure.

More domestic upheavals. Ford, our invaluable maid of all work, has been increasingly absent-minded lately. One day I opened my cupboard to find she had hung all Jim's pressed trousers in it. My dresses were wedged in among Jim's dress shirts in his dressing-room. I taxed her with this, and a host of other minor complaints. She burst into floods of tears, poor thing, and confessed all. Her young man, Bob, who does the post round, has asked her to marry him. They have been stepping out together for years now, and he seems a personable lad. But he wants her to leave our service, and help his old mother run her laundry. Ford is not at all enthusiastic about that part of the plan. However, as she knows, I will not have married persons in my staff. It only leads to ructions. I told Ford that she must choose between her Bob and Linden Gardens. She barely hesitated. 'Bob for me', she said bravely. So be it. Now I have the bother of finding another maid while Ford works out her notice.

Today, Ford forgot to put the tea in the teapot — this being one of the effects of her leaving us on the 15th to be married on the 19th December. Providentially, Lady Peile is turning off one of her maids, Alice, as part of her economy campaign. Lost no time in securing her.

We read that there is plague and famine in India, and wonder how Lily is getting on.

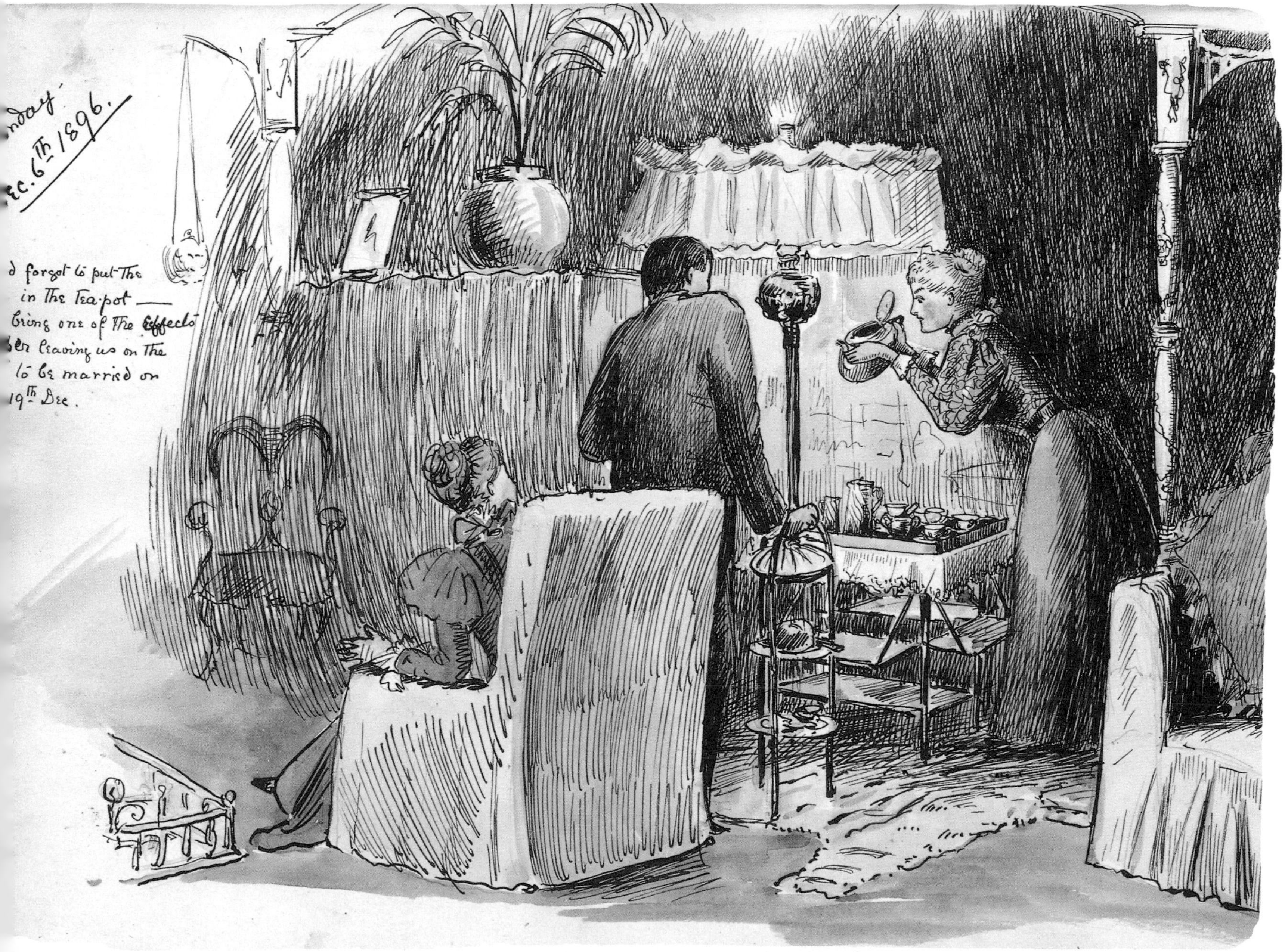

The Patter of Tiny Feet

1897 to 1901

January to June 1897

The Jubilee Year has dawned, with promise of rich celebrations to mark fifty years of Queen Victoria's rule. What a pity Prince Albert is not able to see this day dawn. Feel certain he is looking down from on high with a benign smile. Went to church, called on Mrs Blair, and had tea with Uncle George. Later, Trixie and Jim and I read and sewed in front of the fire.

February

Went on a dizzy shopping spree with Trixie. Such an invaluable companion. She is always willing to fall in with others' plans, having none of her own. Decided I could no longer wear my fur-trimmed cape. Notting Hill Gate must be as deadly bored with it as I am. So we took the omnibus to Bond

Feb. 1st 1897.
"Dumb Crambo"
or choosing an out-door-garment at Fenwicks - Bond St

Evening of New Years Day 1897.
Church in morning. Called on Mrs. Blair in afternoon & afterwards had Tea with Uncle George.

4 Linden Gardens.

Street, and paid a call to Fenwick's. Such an agreeable shop, and you can have tea afterwards in their tea-shop. They have the most delicious Battenburg cake. Did not like any of the coats the young ladies modelled, however, so Notting Hill Gate must bear the fur-trimmed cape a little longer.

March

Decided to remodel all the lace curtains, wash them and mend them. This was a most ambitious project, which took us, in all, two weeks. We lived by day in a swathe of net; by night we dreamt of being smothered in lace. It all began, because I wanted to use the sewing-machine I bought in a sale. Still not quite sure how it works.

May

Jim gave us a dress rehearsal of the part he is to play in the Jubilee celebrations. Now he is a General, he has become very top-lofty, I tease him. The Peiles' children were present and much enjoyed the treat. Jim and his old regiment are to have pride of place among the soldiers lining the Royal way, when the Queen drives through the streets of London to mark the day of her accession next month.

June

Trixie and I have sewed an enormous banner, which we mean to hang from the windows of Linden Gardens. On a white ground, red letters exhort passers-by: 'Jump for Jubilee June Joy'. I am rather proud of that motto. It came to me in the middle of the night, while I was lying awake, listening to Jim's steady breathing. Sad that Lily is

Jubilee Decorations
June. 1897.
Holding Mr. Spencer's coat while he hangs out of the window to nail up the drapery.

not here to enjoy the fun.
Trixie tries hard to be gay, but her sober mien betrays her. She does not really enter into the spirit of things. I think secretly she disapproves of the whole jamboree caboodle. Mr Spencer, an admirer of hers, almost fell out of the window when he was nailing up our effort.

Trixie and I have joined a committee of ladies whose aim is to promote the Jubilee spirit.
To this end, we are organizing a Jubilee Fête for the children of our parish in Kensington Gardens. It requires a great deal of work. We have racked our brains to think up interesting and lively competitions and games to entertain the children. I thought up the Bun Competition. I am rather pleased by the satisfaction it has given to all.

You pierce six buns and thread through the hole a string which you knot. Then you add a small piece of paper on which you write a large number to each bun. Then you hang these six buns from a pole. Only six children have the winning numbers and get a bun to eat. We used to play this to great effect at the Bible Class Picnic in Sandown.
Mrs Pope never failed to draw a parallel with the sermon of loaves and fishes.

The Bun Compctition was a moderate success. London children are rather ill-mannered, I discovered. The six lucky recipients of the buns were kicked and scratched, and the buns trampled into the ground before we managed to restore a semblance of order to the proceedings.

29th June. 1897
Children's Jubilee Fête
Kensington Palace Field.
Bun Competition.

February to August 1898

n interesting event is due to take lace in early March. I am so eavy, I can scarcely move about the house. Very busy making the new arrival's nursery as pleasant an experience as possible. Spent January painting a frieze of lambs gambolling in a meadow round the room. This month, Trixie and I have been making the flounces for the crib. We will not know whether to tie love-knots of pink or of blue satin ribbon round the edges till the day itself.

Jim is worried that I get so little fresh air He was walking in the Park, fretting about this, when he saw an elderly gentleman pulling a Bath-chair up the rise. Jim stopped the man and introduced himself as the husband of a lady in a delicate situation. The gentleman introduced himself as one

Feb. 16th 1898
My first introduction
To a Bath-chair
and Mr. Shelvey
J.C.B. helping up the hills.

Palm Sunday April 3-
3 weeks old.
Dorothy's début.
Dorothy's first toy
May.
April 25th
Dorothy Sackville made a Christian.

Mr Shelvey, retired from the grocery business. He pulled his Bath-chair round the Park from a disinclination to sit at home all day, and on the off-chance that just such a one as Jim might approach him.

So a bargain was struck, the treat was arranged, and today I took my first airing in the Bath-chair. It seemed a very pleasant form of transport, though I worried about the pain my vast weight might be causing Mr Shelvey. I felt pleasantly rested and rocked to a comfortable slumber. I imagined I enjoyed a sensation not unlike that of travellers who take gondolas down the Grand Canal of Venice.

March

Dorothy Sackville Berkeley was born today and is as perfect a little babe as I have ever been privileged to see. Jim the proudest of fathers.

April

Dorothy Sackville made her debut today, it being Palm Sunday. Nurse brought her down to the drawing-room in a fine old array of lace and ribbon. Sir George and Lady Peile were delighted with their new niece, Dorothy gurgled at them both quite happily, just as she does for me, and smiled beautifully at Lady Peile's emerald ring.

Today Dorothy Sackville was made a Christian. A solemn occasion. The vicar looked likely to drop the poor child, it seemed to me in my tremulous state. She began to cry when the vicar approached the font, but hushed when he sprinkled her tiny forehead with holy water. Much moved. Quite soaked my new hat's veiling with my tears. Very jolly party at Linden Gardens afterwards. The cause of the celebration was whisked upstairs by Nurse, and we all drank a great deal of champagne.

May

Jim brought home a most enormous rattle which he had from a street seller. Dorothy hated it and cried till it was taken away. Jim very downcast, but cheered up over a good dinner of roast goose and gooseberry crumble.

June

Every day, Dorothy Sackville grows a little stronger, makes some little progress, at which Nurse and Jim and I exclaim with delight. Today, we short-coated her. Her infant days are over. She has the most adorable red-gold hair which grows apace, and huge blue eyes. I see Jim in her, and he sees me, so we are both content.

Today, a select party of Jim, Nurse, Trixie and I started out for a walk with Dorothy in the perambulator. We all adjured each other to show restraint and caution on our walk. 'Don't coo over the perambulator in public', Jim sternly warned me. He strode along beside us in his most military fashion, saluting acquaintances as we met them.

Trixie, Nurse and I walked in a nervous huddle beside the perambulator. It was he who hailed Mrs Barrymore, and invited her to look at Dorothy. As the old witch in her black bonnet leered over the side of the perambulator, the wee babe began to cry. Who can blame her? Mrs Barrymore looks like Carabosse, the Bad Fairy.

The pleasant stroll in the Park became rather a trial thenceforward. Jim flushed scarlet as Dorothy's howls began to attract other walkers' attention. He quickened his step and strode along at some distance ahead, so no one would think he was with us. Nurse tried to calm Dorothy, and Trixie and I smiled apologetically at passers-by. Very glad to turn for home.

orothy needs far more changes f clothes than I envisaged. ying to keep pace with her equirements. Have made three ight-gowns already. Nurse calls r more. Wonder if she is ot a little fussy in her ways? an Dorothy really need to change er clothes three times a day?

Trying to keep pace with D. S.'s requirements
in the shape of clothes.
June 1898.

ugust

ook Dorothy to Eaton Mascott is summer. It was the greatest ossible success. Rosie and aisy adored her, and spent ours holding her tight little fists nd saying softly, 'Dorothy, orothy, speak to me, Dorothy'. urse learnt, following the ıcksons' Nurse's example, to hange Dorothy only twice a day. ery relieved, as I am very bored ith sewing night-gowns.

1899

Mr Shelvey and his Bath-chair have been an invaluable aid to me again this summer. He has told me much about the grocery business, as well as transporting me about. Promised him to look out for tarantula spiders and other menaces which, he tells me, haunt bunches of bananas. Another interesting event is due to take place in July, to Jim's great pleasure. Sad to lose Trixie. She is off to India to join Lily. Glad that there will be a tiny replacement.

Summered at Sandown, despite Maurice Hamilton Berkeley's arrival in July. A sweet child, small blue eyes, ruddy cheeks, and dark brown hair. Dorothy seems very fond of him, not at all jealous. Had to stop her from throwing toys she does not like into the crib. 'Baby's', she insists, and launches three toy soldiers within an inch of baby's head. Nurse is a great strength at these trying times.

Our move to Cheltenham a mistake. Very stuffy air. Ethel and Nannie visited us in the autumn. Grandmama took a great liking to Dorothy, and we had great games. The old and the young get on very well, but all the company Cheltenham can provide for me is a selection of battered Major-Generals and some ladies who seem too refined to breathe.

Ethel & I find That-
Half an hour of 'See-saw
Margery Daw
is somewhat satisfying'
"more, more"
2 Douro Villas
Cheltenham. Nov. 9th 1899

When Baby is Asleep.

They knew not whence the tyrant came,
They did not even know his name;
Yet he compelled them one and all
To bow in bondage to his thrall;
And from their lips allegiance wrung
Although a stranger to their tongue.

Whilst he was wrapped in royal state,
Their hours of toil were long and late;
No moment could they call their own
Within the precincts of the throne;
And when they dreamed their work was o'er
He only made them slave the more.

Although the conquering king was he
Of people who had once been free,
No word of praise or promise fell
From him his subjects served so well;
And none of those who crowned him lord
Received a shadow of reward.

Obedience to his behest
Destroyed their peace, disturbed their rest;
Yet when his drowsy eyes grew dim,
No mortal dared to waken him—
They stole about with stealthy tread—
"The baby is asleep," they said.

Going to The Post with Grannie's letter.

"Where's Dodderly-"

1900-1

First year of a new century. What will it bring? Nothing in particular. Dorothy and Maurice growing steadily, Jim and I bumbling along as usual.

1901

A new arrival, Malcolm, joined our happy home in February. Suffered terribly, while carrying him, from the icy Bournemouth breezes. Malcolm seems, none the less, extremely bonny and healthy. He has light brown hair—a good head of it—and grey-blue eyes. Dorothy and Maurice are both keenly interested in baby. Dorothy likes to hold him, with a little help from Nurse, and recites her nursery rhymes to him by the hour.

A photograph of my three darling children marks the end of my diary-writing. I am now going to turn my attention to compiling an album for each one. Devoting all my time at present to teaching Dorothy to read. Perhaps one day she, too, will write her diary. As yet, she has difficulty in spelling the simplest of words.

Looking at "The Tortoise" Douro Road, Cheltenham
May 1900.

Dorothy Sackville Berkeley — 4 years
Maurice Hamilton —, 2 yrs. 9 months
Malcolm Spencer —, 1 year 2 months

Epilogue

So what happened next? After the pleasures and pangs of Maud's story up to the end of the century, I was curious to know the sequel. I feel sure that all her readers will also want to know what came next. The very last picture in the last diary, in particular, whetted my appetite for more. Here are Maud's three small children, Dorothy, Maurice and Malcolm, in 1904, aged five, four and two, photographed with 'Noonie', their 'New Nannie'. Noonie looks as if butter wouldn't melt in her mouth: imposing hat, hair smoothly parted in the centre, half smile, starched apron, tightly belted narrow waist. But seventy-three years later Dorothy herself was to make sure that we did not run away with the wrong idea. 'New Nannie a genuine sadist' she wrote across the photograph. I have no doubt that the sadistic nanny of Edward VIII and George VI when children was just such a taut smiling figure. Thanks to the researches of Maud's great-granddaughter, Lorraine Wood, among family albums and papers, we are assured that the sequel was a spirited and suitably adventurous one.

Despite their Noonie, the three young Berkeleys had a cosy happy childhood. The family moved from 4 Linden Gardens, whose typically London view of brick walls and chimney-pots Maud disliked, to Cheltenham, fabled home of retired colonels. However, they both hated the climate of Cheltenham and moved again to Bournemouth, where retired people also congregated, and where the youngest, Malcolm was born. General Berkeley died in 1926 and Maud spent many of the ensuing years with Dorothy, her only daughter.

Dorothy Berkeley had grown up to be as witty and articulate as her parents with a recognized gift for short-story writing. She contributed to Blackwood's and Chambers magazines and to the post-war Penguin Modern Writers series. She wrote one novel. At twenty she married Major Charles Carus-Wilson, an architect and sculptor, and member of the well-known Gloucestershire family. For a while Dorothy and Charles lived in Santiago, Chile, where Charles was working. It was here that Anita was born, their only child and Maud's only grandchild. When Dorothy, Charles and Anita later lived in Austria, Maud joined them and learned the hazards of tobogganing; in Scotland she went camping with them. She settled in Sherborne, Dorset, where the reaper did not come for her, as she would have put it, until she had reached the splendid age of ninety.

Her younger son Malcolm was to die in the same year as Maud, 1949. His remarkable talents were concentrated upon wildlife, among his pets being a cobra in India who sat up at the breakfast-table for a bowl of milk, and in Africa a lion cub who slept on his bed. His friends appreciated Malcolm's charm and sense of humour but were not so fond of his pets. He served in the King's African Rifles in World War II and later was responsible for 'Treetops', the romantic Kenyan hotel built in the branches of a wild fig tree growing beside an animals' drinking pool. Three years after Malcolm's death there took place the most famous event in the history of Treetops. It was here that Princess Elizabeth and Prince Philip, at the start of their visit to Kenya, heard of the death of her father King George VI.

Maud's elder son Maurice was in the 1/7th Gurkha Rifles in India, being stationed first at Sandeman, then in Shilong in Assam, lastly in Rawalpindi. He spent some years training the Gilgit Scouts. In 1940 he was promoted to Lieutenant-Colonel and asked to form a special unit of the Gurkhas at Bakloh, which became the 4/4th. In 1944 he was invalided home with 'sprue', a tropical intestinal disease, and his wife Mollie Reiss, whom he had married seventeen years before, was also seriously ill. They lived in Avening, Gloucestershire. Maurice occupying himself with a local job in Civil Defence. Lorraine Wood, his great-niece, remembers him for playing the piano exceptionally well and being altogether a most entertaining great-uncle. He died of a stroke in 1963.

Maud's grandchild, Anita, was to marry an American lawyer, Joe Wood. This gave her mother Dorothy the chance to visit America and write about it with characteristic sparkle. She too died of a stroke, but not till 1984, and is remembered by Anita's three daughters, Lorraine, Rachel and Helen, as 'a wonderful grandmother'.

One of the most fascinating things that finally emerges from Maud's family story is its continuity within change. The changes are obvious, if transport alone is considered. The young Maud walked all over the Isle of Wight on 'Shanks's pony', as people whimsically called their own two legs. Eventually she succumbed to the lure of 'modern' speed and comfort, but wisely not before the 'penny-farthing' had evolved into the bicycle. During her pregnancies, though, it was still the antiquated Bath-chair that kept her going. The continuity comes through in Maud's descendants. The Tomlinsons and Berkeleys were the kind of families who would unerringly find their way, generation after generation, to the Antipodes or into the Raj, which they would faithfully support in its last struggle. When there was no longer a 'Jewel in the Crown' to guard, they would scatter all over the world before coming home, or fly symbolically onward and upward into Treetops.

Miss Francis,
('Noonie' short for 'New Nannie'
a genuine Sadist
Dec 1977
Baby, Dorothy, Maurice
Sept. 1904

ud happily took to her new role as a mother, in her forties, providing ar Jim' with a second family

In the 'jungle' garden at Rahere, Bournemouth. Left to right, Dorothy: 9 years 5 months, Malcolm: 6 years 6 months and Maurice: 8 years 2 months

Maurice and 'JCB' in 1909

Family group taken in 1909 in Bournemouth

Dorothy at 6 years old

1907. -Bournemouth-
Cricket.
Rahere. Sept. 1907.

1907 -Bournemouth-

Maud fulfilled her promise to record her children's development by compiling a charming and witty album for each one. She was affectionately known as 'Guy' by younger members of the family, and her sense of humour remained intact even at the age of eighty-seven

Patience
Poor Guy!
M. B.
These cards are absolute
" I can't make them come out
Right.
1946.